Sister Schubert's

Secret

BREAD
RECIPES

Sister Schubert's
Secret
BREAD
RECIPES

Oxmoor
House®

Library of Congress Catalog Number: 96-68890
ISBN: 0-8487-1517-9
Manufactured in the United States of America
Second Printing 1997

Editor-in-Chief: Nancy Fitzpatrick Wyatt
Editorial Director, Special Interest Publications: Ann H. Harvey
Senior Foods Editor: Susan Carlisle Payne
Senior Editor, Editorial Services: Olivia Kindig Wells
Art Director: James Boone

Sister Schubert's Secret Bread Recipes

Editor: Lisa Hooper Talley
Assistant Editor: Kelly Hooper Troiano
Copy Editor: Jacqueline B. Giovanelli
Editorial Assistants: Julie A. Cole, Allison Ingram
Director, Test Kitchens: Kathleen Royal Phillips
Assistant Director, Test Kitchens: Gayle Hays Sadler
Test Kitchens Home Economists: Susan Hall Bellows, Julie Christopher, Michele Brown Fuller,
        Heather Irby, Natalie E. King, Elizabeth Tyler Luckett, Jan Jacks Moon,
        Iris Crawley O'Brien, Jan A. Smith
Associate Art Director: Cynthia R. Cooper
Designer: Rita Yerby
Photographer: Jim Bathie
Photo Stylist: Kay E. Clarke
Publishing Systems Administrator: Rick Tucker
Director, Production and Distribution: Phillip Lee
Associate Production Manager: Vanessa Cobbs Richardson
Production Coordinator: Marianne Jordan Wilson
Production Assistant: Valerie Heard

Front Cover: *Parkerhouse Rolls (page 10), Cinnamon Rolls (page 12), Orange Rolls (page 13)*
Back Cover: *Sausage Rolls (page 11), Sister's Jalapeño Cornbread (page 69)*
Page 2 (front to back): *Applesauce Bread (page 100), Glazed Orange Scones (page 49),*
    Muffins Tropicale (page 55)

Contents

SISTER SCHUBERT: ON A ROLL!

Music sets the pace at the bakery in Luverne, Alabama, where approximately 135,000 rolls a day bake in large revolving ovens. Every phase of production at Sister Schubert's Homemade Rolls is state-of-the-art: From the assembly line where the rolls are formed, to the proofing room where they rise in an environment of precisely-controlled temperature and humidity, to the icy blast freezer where the rolls are flash frozen.

But not so long ago, in 1989, Sister Schubert baked her famous rolls in the kitchen of her home in Troy, Alabama, just for family and friends. That same year, Sister donated a few pans of Parkerhouse rolls to her church's holiday frozen food fair. The rolls were such a popular item that she received orders for 80 additional pans.

The following year, Sister had to cut off the orders at 200 pans, and the next year, she stopped at 300 pans. Her whole family joined in the effort to get the rolls out. Sister remembers, "I sat down after that third holiday fair and said to myself, 'If the people in Troy like my rolls, maybe other folks will too.'"

In no time, Sister bought two professional ovens, a small chest freezer, and a 30-quart professional mixer. The sun room of her home became a mini bakery, complete with a plastic flap door to keep the humidity and heat in the room correctly balanced. The dining room table served as a cooling and packaging area. With help from her daughters, Charlotte and Chrissie, other enthusiastic family members, and three coworkers, Sister began her fledgling business with one account, Ingram's Curb Market in Troy.

After just one month, Sister was delivering 120 pans of rolls a week to the small neighborhood grocery. Her next objective was to introduce her rolls to new markets, so she called on several small groceries in southern Alabama. "I knew," Sister says, "that if I could just get people to taste my rolls, they would want to buy them." She and her daughters, decked out in Sister's signature green and white aprons, handed out samples of Parkerhouse rolls at the markets. Sister's prediction was right—folks who tasted the rolls wanted to buy them.

With orders coming in faster than they could be filled, the next challenge was expansion. Sister took her dreams and her rolls to a Troy banker for help. He tasted, they talked, and soon Sister Schubert's Homemade Rolls was on its way to a new home.

The first official bakery was located in 1,000 square feet of space in her family's furniture warehouse, expanding to 2,000 square feet within one month. Then Sister finally took over the entire warehouse.

"Those were busy, exciting days," recalls Sister. "Many times we were working around the clock, up to our elbows in flour and icing. We were growing so fast and had so much to learn about the business that it seemed as if we took three steps forward and two steps back some days."

Again and again, demand for Sister's rolls far exceeded production. Major grocery stores began placing large orders, and soon, Sister Schubert's Homemade Rolls was on its way to the new, high-tech bakery in Luverne, Alabama, that still houses the business.

Today, Sister Schubert's homemade rolls are shipped to 1,300 stores in 18 states. And just like the bakery, the product line, too, has grown. The star of Sister's line will always be the original Parkerhouse Rolls, but Cinnamon Rolls, Orange Rolls, Sausage Rolls, and Sourdough Rolls are customer favorites, too. Her line also includes Sister's Southern Cornbread and Sister's Jalapeño Cornbread.

Sister credits her family, her coworkers, and her faith for the phenomenal success she has experienced in such a short time. But those who work with her will be the first to say that Sister Schubert's tireless enthusiasm for the quality of her products is the key to her success.

Many heartfelt thanks to my sister Charlotte for helping me recall the wonderful memories of our childhood as we compiled the recipes for this book.

Sister

SISTER'S SPECIALTIES

*T*he first time I ever made my Parkerhouse Rolls was for Thanksgiving dinner with my family and friends. I was nervous about the whole idea of making yeast rolls because the technique was new to me. But the rolls came out of the oven golden and light with an aroma that called everyone to the table before I could ring the dinner bell.

Because of this first success, Parkerhouse Rolls became the charter member of my product line. From that original recipe for Parkerhouse Rolls came variations for other favorites—Cinnamon Rolls, Orange Rolls, and Sausage Rolls. In addition to the recipes for these rolls, I've included family recipes for Sourdough Rolls and Sourdough Starter in this chapter.

Grandmother Wood gave me the original recipe for Parkerhouse Rolls, which came from a cook in her mother's family. I don't know the cook's name, but I think she'd be pleased to know that so many people are enjoying her rolls after all these years.

PARKERHOUSE ROLLS

(pictured on page 19 and on front cover)

The secret to the light–as–a–feather texture of these rolls: Don't knead the dough!

❧ For this recipe, sift the flour into a large bowl before measuring out the amount called for. Turn to pages 20 and 21 for step–by–step instructions for making Parkerhouse Rolls.

1	package active dry yeast
1½	cups warm water (105° to 115°)
5	cups sifted all-purpose flour, divided
½	cup sugar
1½	teaspoons salt
½	cup shortening, melted
2	large eggs, lightly beaten
½	cup butter, melted
1¼	cups all-purpose flour

Combine yeast and warm water in a 2-cup liquid measuring cup; let stand 5 minutes.

Combine 4 cups sifted flour, sugar, and salt in a large bowl. Stir in yeast mixture and shortening. Add eggs and remaining 1 cup sifted flour; stir vigorously until well blended. (Dough will be soft and sticky.) Brush or lightly rub dough with some of the melted butter. Cover loosely; let rise in a warm place (85°), free from drafts, 1½ hours or until doubled in bulk.

Grease 4 (8-inch) round cakepans; set aside.

Sift ¾ cup flour in a thick layer evenly over work surface; turn dough out onto floured surface. (Dough will be soft.) Sift ½ cup flour evenly over dough. Roll dough to ½-inch thickness; brush off excess flour.

Cut out dough using a floured 2-inch biscuit cutter. Pull each round into an oval, approximately 2½ inches long. Dip 1 side of oval into melted butter. Fold oval in half with buttered side facing out. (Floured side will form the famous Parkerhouse pocket.)

For each pan, place the folds of 10 rolls against side of

prepared pan, pressing center fronts of rolls together gently to seal. Place 5 rolls in inner circle, and 1 roll in center for a total of 16 rolls per pan. Cover loosely, and let rise in a warm place, free from drafts, 1 hour or until doubled in bulk.

Preheat oven to 400°. Bake rolls, uncovered, for 12 to 15 minutes or until lightly browned. Yield: 64 rolls.

SAUSAGE ROLLS

(pictured on back cover)

This variation of Parkerhouse Rolls contains a savory surprise— smoked cocktail sausages.

64   smoked cocktail sausages
1   recipe Parkerhouse Rolls dough (facing page)

Place sausages in a single layer in a shallow pan. Bake at 350° for 20 minutes. Drain well on paper towels.

To assemble, fold the buttered cut-out dough for Parkerhouse Rolls around the cooked sausages before placing rolls in the prepared pans. Continue preparing rolls as directed in Parkerhouse Rolls recipe. Yield: 64 rolls.

Baking the sausages before inserting them in the rolls keeps the sausages from making the rolls greasy.

HERB BUTTER

1   cup butter, softened
1   tablespoon sesame seeds
2   teaspoons celery seeds
2   teaspoons poppy seeds
⅛   teaspoon garlic powder

Combine all ingredients. Gently brush butter mixture over tops of Parkerhouse Rolls (facing page) or Sourdough Rolls (page 14) after second rising, just before baking. Yield: 1 cup.

CINNAMON ROLLS

(pictured on front cover)

1	cup sugar
1	cup butter, melted
½	cup ground cinnamon
1	recipe Parkerhouse Rolls dough (page 10)
1½	cups all-purpose flour, divided
½	cup butter, melted
2½	cups sifted powdered sugar
¼	cup milk
1	teaspoon vanilla

Combine first 3 ingredients; set aside. Grease 4 (8-inch) round cakepans; set aside.

After Parkerhouse Rolls dough has risen per directions, sift ½ cup flour in a thick layer evenly over work surface. Turn half of dough out onto floured surface. (Dough will be very soft.) Set remaining half of dough aside.

Sift ¼ cup flour evenly over dough. Roll dough into a 30-x 20-inch rectangle. Spread half of cinnamon mixture over dough. Roll up dough jellyroll fashion, starting at the short side, just to the center of the rectangle; cut dough along side of roll to release it. Roll up remaining half of rectangle in the same fashion. Set rolls of dough aside. Repeat procedure using remaining ¾ cup flour, dough, and cinnamon mixture.

Cut each roll of dough into 16 (1¼-inch-thick) slices. Place 16 slices, cut sides down, in each prepared pan, leaving ¼-inch space between slices. Brush slices with ½ cup melted butter. Let rise, uncovered, in a warm place (85°), free from drafts, 1 hour or until doubled in bulk.

Preheat oven to 375°. Bake rolls, uncovered, for 15 to 18 minutes or until lightly browned. Cool slightly in pans on wire racks. Combine powdered sugar, milk, and vanilla, stirring until smooth; drizzle over warm rolls. Yield: 64 rolls.

ORANGE ROLLS

(pictured on front cover)

2	cups sugar
1	cup butter, melted
¾	cup coarsely grated orange rind (5 oranges)
1	recipe Parkerhouse Rolls dough (page 10)
1½	cups all-purpose flour, divided
½	cup butter, melted
2½	cups sifted powdered sugar
¼	cup fresh orange juice
½	cup coarsely grated orange rind (3 oranges)

Combine first 3 ingredients; set aside. Grease 4 (8-inch) round cakepans; set aside.

After Parkerhouse Rolls dough has risen per directions, sift ½ cup flour in a thick layer evenly over work surface. Turn half of dough out onto floured surface. (Dough will be very soft.) Set remaining half of dough aside.

Sift ¼ cup flour evenly over dough. Roll dough into a 30- x 20-inch rectangle. Spread half of orange rind mixture over dough. Roll up dough jellyroll fashion, starting at the short side, just to the center of the rectangle; cut dough along side of roll to release it. Roll up remaining half of rectangle in the same fashion. Set rolls of dough aside. Repeat procedure using remaining ¾ cup flour, dough, and orange rind mixture.

Cut each roll of dough into 16 (1¼-inch-thick) slices. Place 16 slices, cut sides down, in each prepared pan, leaving ¼-inch space between slices. Brush slices with ½ cup melted butter. Let rise, uncovered, in a warm place (85°), free from drafts, 1 hour or until doubled in bulk.

Preheat oven to 375°. Bake rolls, uncovered, for 15 to 18 minutes or until lightly browned. Cool slightly in pans on wire racks. Combine powdered sugar, orange juice, and ½ cup orange rind; drizzle over warm rolls. Yield: 64 rolls.

There's no substitute for the exceptional taste of fresh orange rind in this recipe. Avoid grating any stamped or marked areas of skin on the oranges. Also avoid grating into the bitter white pith of the orange.

SOURDOUGH ROLLS

Mama introduced me to baking with sourdough. She even made the starter that we still use at the bakery today.

Sourdough Starter (facing page) is alive and growing. Always cover it loosely so that it can get oxygen.

1½	cups warm water (105° to 115°)
1	cup Sourdough Starter (facing page)
½	cup shortening, melted and cooled to 105° to 115°
6	cups all-purpose flour
1	teaspoon salt
½	cup butter, melted

Combine first 3 ingredients in a large bowl. Combine flour and salt in a large bowl. Stir 5 cups of flour mixture into starter mixture. Using your hands, incorporate remaining 1 cup flour mixture. Cover loosely, and let rise in a warm place (85°), free from drafts, 8 hours.

Grease 4 (8-inch) round cakepans; set aside.

Punch dough down; turn out onto a well-floured surface, and knead 10 times. Divide dough in half.

Roll 1 portion of dough to ½-inch thickness; cut into 32 rounds using a floured 2-inch biscuit cutter. Pull each round into an oval, approximately 2½ inches long. Dip 1 side of oval into melted butter. Fold oval in half with buttered side facing out.

For each pan, place the folds of 10 rolls against side of prepared pan, pressing center fronts of rolls together gently to seal. Place 5 rolls in inner circle, and 1 roll in center of pan for a total of 16 rolls per pan. Repeat entire procedure with remaining half of dough.

Cover loosely, and let rise in a warm place, free from drafts, 6 hours or until doubled in bulk.

Preheat oven to 375°. Bake rolls, uncovered, for 15 to 18 minutes or until lightly browned. Yield: 64 rolls.

Sourdough Starter

2	packages active dry yeast
1½	cups warm water (105° to 115°), divided
⅔	cup sugar
3	tablespoons instant potato flakes

Combine yeast and ½ cup warm water in a 1-cup liquid measuring cup; let stand 5 minutes.

Combine yeast mixture, remaining 1 cup warm water, sugar, and potato flakes in a large bowl, stirring until well blended. Cover loosely, and let stand in a warm place (85°), free from drafts, 8 hours. (Starter is ready to use at this point.) Refrigerate starter after 8 hours.

Feed Sourdough Starter Every 3 Days With:

1	cup warm water (105° to 115°)
⅔	cup sugar
3	tablespoons instant potato flakes

After feeding starter, cover loosely, and let stand in a warm place (85°), free from drafts, 8 hours. Refrigerate starter after 8 hours.

Sister's Secret

The temperature of the water is critical in making Sourdough Starter. Use a candy thermometer to be sure that the water isn't too hot.

CHEDDAR ROLLS

1   (8-ounce) package New York sharp
        Cheddar cheese
2   pans baked Parkerhouse Rolls
        (page 10) or Sourdough Rolls (page 14)

Slice cheese crosswise into 16 strips; slice strips in half. Open each roll, and place 1 cheese piece in center; close rolls. Return rolls to pans; cover loosely with aluminum foil. Bake at 350° for 15 minutes or until cheese is melted. Serve warm. Yield: 32 rolls.

MEDITERRANEAN ROLLS

8   ounces crumbled feta cheese
⅓   cup mayonnaise
¼   cup chopped sun-dried tomatoes in oil
2   teaspoons chopped fresh basil or
        ¾ teaspoon dried basil
½   teaspoon pepper
2   pans baked Parkerhouse Rolls
        (page 10) or Sourdough Rolls (page 14)

Combine first 5 ingredients. Open each roll, and spread each with about 1 teaspoon cheese mixture; close rolls. Return rolls to pans; cover loosely with aluminum foil. Bake at 350° for 15 minutes or until thoroughly heated. Serve warm. Yield: 32 rolls.

TENDERLOIN ROLLS

1   cup sour cream
⅓   cup prepared horseradish
1   tablespoon lemon juice
¼   teaspoon salt
2   pans baked Parkerhouse Rolls
        (page 10) or Sourdough Rolls (page 14)
1   pound cooked beef tenderloin,
        thinly sliced

Combine first 4 ingredients. Open each roll, and spread each with 2 teaspoons sour cream mixture. Place slices of tenderloin over sour cream mixture; close rolls. Return rolls to pans; cover loosely with aluminum foil. Bake at 350° for 15 to 20 minutes or until thoroughly heated. Serve warm. Yield: 32 rolls.

TURKEY ROLLS

2   pans baked Parkerhouse Rolls
        (page 10) or Sourdough Rolls (page 14)
1   (8-ounce) jar orange marmalade
1   pound cooked turkey, thinly sliced

Open each roll, and spread each with 1½ teaspoons orange marmalade. Place a slice of turkey over marmalade; close rolls. Return rolls to pans; cover loosely with aluminum foil. Bake at 350° for 15 to 20 minutes or until thoroughly heated. Serve warm. Yield: 32 rolls.

Freezing & Reheating Techniques

Each recipe for my signature rolls makes 4 pans of rolls. It's easy and convenient to freeze and reheat the rolls. Simply follow these step–by–step instructions for just–baked flavor every time.

Microwaving is not recommended as a reheating method for these rolls.

To bake rolls: Prepare rolls according to recipe, baking only 8 to 10 minutes or just until rolls begin to brown. Remove rolls from oven, and let cool completely in pans on wire racks.

Note: For Cinnamon Rolls and Orange Rolls, drizzle icing over cooled rolls; let stand 20 to 25 minutes or until icing hardens slightly before placing pans in bags.

To freeze rolls: Place each pan of cooled rolls in a 13½-x 11-inch food storage and freezer bag with a twist tie or in a large zip-top freezer bag. (Food storage and freezer bags with twist ties are a perfect fit for the 9-inch pans, and allow little air circulation.) Seal bags. Place pans in a single layer in freezer until frozen. (The pans may be stacked after the rolls are frozen.) Freeze up to 3 months.

To reheat frozen rolls: Preheat oven to 300°. Remove pan from freezer bag, and cover pan loosely with aluminum foil. Place pan on center rack of oven, and bake 20 minutes. Uncover and bake 10 to 15 additional minutes or until lightly browned.

To reheat thawed rolls: Allow rolls to thaw in the freezer bag in the refrigerator 8 hours or overnight. Preheat oven to 350°. Remove pan from bag, and place pan, uncovered, on center rack of oven. Bake 15 to 20 minutes or until lightly browned.

Parkerhouse Rolls (page 10)

TECHNIQUES FOR PREPARING PARKERHOUSE ROLLS

1. Allow the dough for Parkerhouse Rolls (page 10) to rise until doubled in size. (Because the dough is so soft, this will take 1½ to 2 hours). Before kneading the dough, place ¾ cup flour in a sifter, and sift the flour evenly in a thick layer over the work surface.

2. Turn the soft dough out onto the floured surface; sift ½ cup additional flour evenly over the dough. (Do not knead the dough.) Roll the dough to ½-inch thickness, and brush off any excess flour.

3. Cut the dough into rounds using a floured 2-inch biscuit cutter, cutting the rounds as close together as possible. Lightly press the remnants of dough together, and reroll to ½-inch thickness; cut the dough into rounds.

4. Gently stretch each round of dough into an oval about 2½ inches long. Dip 1 side of each oval in melted butter, and fold in half with the buttered side facing out. (The floured side forms the famous Parkerhouse pocket.)

5. For each pan, place the folds of 10 rolls against the side of the greased pan, pressing the center fronts of the rolls together gently to seal. Place 5 rolls in the next circle, and place 1 roll in the center for 16 rolls per pan.

6. Cover the rolls loosely, and let them rise 1 hour or until doubled in size. After the rolls rise, bake them at 400° for 12 to 15 minutes or until lightly browned. See page 18 for convenient freezing and reheating instructions. ✍

ROLLS

Whether they're tender and buttery sweet or crusty and studded with bran, rolls are an essential part of our Southern dining experience. My grandmother's notebooks listed an amazing number of recipes for rolls, so choosing which ones to include in this collection was a difficult (but delicious) process.

I finally narrowed down the selection to those I remembered being my favorites—sweet Butterscotch Rolls, pungent Herb Rolls, and hearty Bran Rolls. You'll also find recipes for soft pan rolls, plump dinner rolls, cloverleaf rolls, and crescents.

Be creative when you make these wonderful old recipes your own, thus continuing the happy tradition of great bakers and grandmothers everywhere.

Front to back: *Bran Rolls (Page 32), Herb Rolls (Page 29)*

Everlasting Rolls

This recipe was one of my grandmother's favorites. In her version of the recipe, ingredients were listed in "heaping" pints and "scant" quarts instead of in cups. Also, she called for the dough to be "taken up" and "pushed down" and for the baking to be done in a "quick" oven. It was an adventure to translate everything for today's baker.

> ☙ This dough will keep, tightly covered, in your refrigerator up to one week. Remember to allow time for the dough to rise after it has chilled.

2	cups milk
½	cup sugar
½	cup shortening
2	packages active dry yeast
6	cups all-purpose flour, divided
1½	teaspoons salt
1	teaspoon baking powder
1	teaspoon baking soda
½	cup butter, melted

Combine first 3 ingredients in a saucepan; heat until shortening melts, stirring occasionally. Cool to 105° to 115°. Add yeast; stir until dissolved. Let stand 5 minutes.

Combine yeast mixture and 2 cups flour in a large bowl. (Mixture will be consistency of thin batter.) Cover loosely, and let rise in a warm place (85°), free from drafts, 2 hours.

Combine remaining 4 cups flour, salt, baking powder, and soda; add to batter, stirring until dough pulls away from sides of bowl. Cover with plastic wrap; refrigerate overnight.

Let dough stand, covered, at room temperature until soft (2 to 2½ hours). Turn dough out onto a well-floured surface; roll to ½-inch thickness. Cut with a floured 1½-inch biscuit cutter. Place rolls on ungreased baking sheets, leaving 1 inch of space between rolls; brush with melted butter. Cover loosely; let rise in a warm place, free from drafts, 2 hours.

Preheat oven to 400°. Bake rolls, uncovered, for 10 to 12 minutes or until lightly browned. Yield: 64 rolls.

LIGHT-AS-A-FEATHER ROLLS

2	cups water
1	medium baking potato, peeled and cubed
2	packages active dry yeast
2	tablespoons shortening
1	cup milk
½	cup sugar
6	cups all-purpose flour, divided
1½	teaspoons salt
½	cup butter, melted

Bring 2 cups water to a boil in a saucepan; add potato, and cook over medium heat 15 minutes or until tender. Drain, reserving cooking liquid. Mash potato, reserving ½ cup mashed potato; set aside. Cool potato liquid to 105° to 115°.

Combine yeast and warm potato liquid in a small bowl; let stand 5 minutes. Add shortening to yeast mixture; stir until melted.

Combine reserved ½ cup mashed potato, milk, and sugar in a large bowl. Add yeast mixture and 2 cups flour, stirring well. Cover loosely, and let rise in a warm place (85°), free from drafts, 2 hours.

Combine remaining 4 cups flour and salt. Add to yeast mixture, 1 cup at a time, stirring well after each addition. Stir until dough pulls away from sides of bowl.

Turn dough out onto a well-floured surface, and roll dough to ½-inch thickness. Cut out dough using a floured 1½-inch biscuit cutter. Pull each round of dough into an oval, approximately 2 inches long. Fold ovals in half; pinch closed at front. Place rolls on greased large baking sheets, leaving 1 inch of space between rolls; brush with melted butter. Cover loosely, and let rise in a warm place, free from drafts, 1 hour or until doubled in bulk.

Preheat oven to 400°. Bake rolls, uncovered, for 12 to 15 minutes or until lightly browned. Yield: 64 rolls.

POCKET ROLLS

This dough will keep in the refrigerator up to one week. Just make sure it's covered tightly with plastic wrap. Let the chilled dough come to room temperature (about two hours) before making the rolls.

2	cups milk
½	cup sugar
½	cup shortening
2	packages active dry yeast
½	cup warm water (105° to 115°)
6	cups all-purpose flour, divided
1	teaspoon baking powder
½	teaspoon baking soda
1½	teaspoons salt
½	cup whipping cream

Combine first 3 ingredients in a saucepan; heat until short-ening melts, stirring occasionally. Cool to 105° to 115°.

Combine yeast and warm water in a 1-cup liquid mea-suring cup; let stand 5 minutes. Combine milk mixture and yeast mixture.

Combine yeast mixture and 4 cups flour in a large bowl. Cover loosely, and let rise in a warm place (85°), free from drafts, 1 hour or until doubled in bulk.

Combine remaining 2 cups flour, baking powder, soda, and salt. Stir dough down; add flour mixture, stirring until dough pulls away from sides of bowl.

Turn dough out onto a well-floured surface, and knead lightly 3 or 4 times. Roll dough to ½-inch thickness; cut out dough using a floured 1½-inch biscuit cutter. Pull each round of dough into an oval, approximately 2 inches long. Fold ovals in half, and pinch closed at the front. Place rolls on greased large baking sheets, leaving 1 inch of space between rolls. Cover loosely, and let rise in a warm place, free from drafts, 45 minutes or until doubled in bulk.

Preheat oven to 400°. Gently brush rolls with whipping cream. Bake for 12 to 15 minutes or until lightly browned. Yield: 64 rolls.

ICEBOX ROLLS

My grandmother's refrigerator, or icebox as she called it, usually contained a batch of these rolls.

2	cups water
¾	cup sugar
¾	cup shortening
2	packages active dry yeast
½	cup warm water (105° to 115°)
7	cups all-purpose flour, divided
2	large eggs, lightly beaten
1½	teaspoons salt
½	cup butter, melted

Combine first 3 ingredients in a large saucepan; heat until shortening melts, stirring occasionally. Cool to 105° to 115°.

Combine yeast and warm water in a 1-cup liquid measuring cup; let stand 5 minutes. Add yeast mixture to mixture in saucepan; stir well.

Combine yeast mixture, 1 cup flour, and eggs in a large bowl. Combine remaining 6 cups flour and salt; stir into yeast mixture, 1 cup at a time, until dough pulls away from sides of bowl. Cover tightly; chill at least 2 hours or overnight.

Let dough stand, covered, at room temperature until soft enough to work with (2 to 2½ hours).

Turn dough out onto a well-floured surface, and knead until smooth and elastic (5 to 7 minutes). Divide dough into fourths. Divide each portion into 16 equal pieces; shape each piece into a ball. Arrange rolls on greased large baking sheets, leaving 1 inch of space between rolls. Brush rolls with melted butter. Cover loosely, and let rise in a warm place (85°), free from drafts, 2 hours or until doubled in bulk.

Preheat oven to 400°. Bake rolls, uncovered, for 12 to 15 minutes or until lightly browned. Yield: 64 rolls.

MILLENNIUM ROLLS

In Grandmother's notebook, these rolls were titled "New Century Rolls," referring to the year 1900. I thought it would be interesting to update the recipe for the year 2000 since good food does endure!

2	packages active dry yeast
2	cups warm milk (105° to 115°)
6	to 6¼ cups all-purpose flour, divided
1	tablespoon sugar
1	teaspoon salt
2	tablespoons shortening, melted
2	large eggs, separated
½	cup butter, melted

Combine yeast and warm milk; let stand 5 minutes.

Combine 4 cups flour, sugar, and salt in a large bowl. Add yeast mixture and melted shortening; stir until well blended. Cover loosely, and let rise in a warm place (85°), free from drafts, 1 hour or until doubled in bulk.

Beat egg yolks at medium speed of an electric mixer until thick and pale. Beat egg whites at high speed until stiff peaks form. Add egg yolks to dough; stir until well blended. Fold in beaten egg whites.

Add remaining 2 cups flour to dough, 1 cup at a time, stirring until dough pulls away from sides of bowl. (Stir in remaining ¼ cup flour, if necessary, to keep dough from being sticky.)

Turn dough out onto a well-floured surface; knead lightly. Divide dough into thirds. Divide each portion into 12 equal pieces; shape each piece into a ball. Arrange rolls on greased large baking sheets, leaving 1 inch of space between rolls; brush with butter. Cover loosely; let rise in a warm place, free from drafts, 45 minutes or until doubled in bulk.

Preheat oven to 375°. Bake rolls, uncovered, for 20 to 25 minutes or until lightly browned. Yield: 3 dozen.

HERB ROLLS

(pictured on page 22)

1	cup milk
¼	cup butter
2¼	to 2½ cups all-purpose flour, divided
⅓	cup rolled oats
⅓	cup sugar
1	package active dry yeast
1	large egg, lightly beaten
¾	cup whole wheat flour
1	teaspoon salt
1	egg white, lightly beaten
2	teaspoons dried Italian seasoning

Combine milk and butter in a saucepan; heat until butter melts, stirring occasionally. Cool to 120° to 130°.

Combine 1 cup all-purpose flour and next 3 ingredients in a large bowl; add milk mixture and 1 egg, stirring well. Add 1¼ cups all-purpose flour, whole wheat flour, and salt, stirring until dough pulls away from sides of bowl.

Turn dough out onto a well-floured surface; knead 5 minutes. (Knead in remaining ¼ cup all-purpose flour, if necessary, to keep dough from being sticky.) Place dough in a well-greased bowl, turning to coat. Cover loosely; let rise in a warm place (85°), free from drafts, 1 hour or until doubled in bulk.

Punch dough down; turn out onto a lightly floured surface, and knead lightly 3 or 4 times. Divide dough into 16 equal pieces; shape each piece into a ball. Arrange rolls in a greased 9-inch square pan, leaving 1 inch of space between rolls. Cover loosely, and let rise in a warm place, free from drafts, 45 minutes or until doubled in bulk.

Preheat oven to 375°. Brush rolls with egg white; sprinkle with Italian seasoning. Bake for 20 to 25 minutes or until rolls are lightly browned. Yield: 16 rolls.

MISS ANN'S ROLLS

Miss Ann was our next-door neighbor for many years. A gourmet cook, she had a lot of influence on my interest in cooking.

Use this dough to make pretzel-shaped or bow-shaped rolls. Divide the dough into 36 equal pieces. Roll each piece of dough into a 9-inch rope; loosely tie into a knot resembling a pretzel. Place on greased baking sheets, leaving 2 inches of space between rolls. Bake as directed.

½	cup water
¼	cup sugar
¼	cup butter
½	cup milk
1	large egg, lightly beaten
1	package active dry yeast
1	teaspoon sugar
¼	cup warm water (105° to 115°)
4	cups all-purpose flour
1½	teaspoons salt
½	cup butter, melted

Combine first 3 ingredients in a saucepan; heat until butter melts, stirring occasionally. (Do not boil.) Remove from heat; stir in milk and egg. Cool to 105° to 115°.

Combine yeast, 1 teaspoon sugar, and warm water in a 1-cup liquid measuring cup; let stand 5 minutes. Combine butter mixture and yeast mixture.

Combine yeast mixture, flour, and salt in a large bowl; stir well. (Dough will be soft.) Brush or rub dough with some of the melted butter. Cover loosely; let rise in a warm place (85°), free from drafts, 1 hour or until doubled in bulk.

Grease 2 (13- x 9- x 2-inch) pans; set aside.

Punch dough down; turn out onto a well-floured surface. Knead lightly 4 or 5 times. Divide dough in half. Divide each half into 12 equal pieces; shape each piece into a ball. Arrange rolls in pans, leaving 1 inch of space between rolls; brush with remaining melted butter. Cover loosely; let rise in a warm place, free from drafts, 45 minutes or until doubled in bulk.

Preheat oven to 400°. Bake rolls, uncovered, for 15 to 20 minutes or until lightly browned. Yield: 2 dozen.

SOUR CREAM ROLLS

4¾	cups all-purpose flour, divided
1	cup potato flakes
2	teaspoons sugar
2	packages active dry yeast
2	cups milk
½	cup sour cream
2	large eggs, lightly beaten
2	teaspoons salt
¼	cup butter, melted

Combine 2 cups flour, potato flakes, sugar, and yeast in a large bowl; set aside.

Combine milk and sour cream in a saucepan; heat until mixture reaches 120° to 130°. Add milk mixture to flour mixture, stirring until well blended. Add eggs; stir well. Add remaining 2¾ cups flour and salt to yeast mixture, stirring until dough pulls away from sides of bowl. Brush or lightly rub dough with some of the melted butter. Cover loosely, and let rise in a warm place (85°), free from drafts, 45 minutes or until doubled in bulk.

Grease 2 (13- x 9- x 2-inch) pans; set aside.

Turn dough out onto a well-floured surface, and knead until smooth and elastic (about 3 minutes). Divide dough in half. Divide each half into 12 equal pieces; shape each piece into a ball. Arrange rolls in prepared pans, leaving 1 inch of space between rolls; brush with remaining butter. Cover loosely; let rise in a warm place, free from drafts, 30 minutes or until doubled in bulk.

Preheat oven to 375°. Bake rolls, uncovered, for 20 to 30 minutes or until lightly browned. Yield: 2 dozen.

Bran Rolls

(pictured on page 22)

1	cup shreds of wheat bran cereal
1	cup water
1	cup butter
¾	cup sugar
2½	packages active dry yeast
1	cup warm water (105° to 115°)
2	large eggs, lightly beaten
7½	cups all-purpose flour
1½	teaspoons salt
½	cup butter, melted

Combine first 4 ingredients in a large saucepan; bring to a boil. Remove from heat; let cool. Transfer mixture to a large bowl.

Combine yeast and 1 cup warm water in a small bowl; let stand 5 minutes. Add yeast mixture and eggs to cereal mixture; stir until well blended.

Combine flour and salt; add to cereal mixture, 1 cup at a time, stirring until dough pulls away from sides of bowl. Brush or lightly rub dough with some of the melted butter. Cover loosely, and let rise in a warm place (85°), free from drafts, 1 hour or until doubled in bulk.

Punch dough down; turn out onto a well-floured surface. Divide dough into thirds; divide each third into 12 equal pieces. Divide each piece again into 3 equal pieces. Shape each piece into a ball. Place 3 balls in each of 36 greased muffin cups, forming cloverleaf rolls; brush with remaining melted butter. Cover loosely, and let rise in a warm place, free from drafts, 45 minutes or until doubled in bulk.

Preheat oven to 375°. Bake rolls, uncovered, for 20 to 25 minutes or until lightly browned. Remove from pans immediately. Yield: 3 dozen.

CRESCENT ROLLS

1	package active dry yeast
1	cup warm water (105° to 115°)
1	cup sugar
1	teaspoon salt
3	large eggs, lightly beaten
4½	cups all-purpose flour
½	cup butter, softened and divided

Combine yeast and warm water in a 1-cup liquid measuring cup; let stand 5 minutes.

Combine yeast mixture, sugar, salt, and eggs in a large bowl. Add flour; stir until dough pulls away from bowl.

Turn dough out onto a well-floured surface, and knead 5 minutes. Place in a well-greased bowl, turning to grease top. Cover loosely, and let rise in a warm place (85°), free from drafts, 1 hour or until doubled in bulk.

Punch dough down; turn out onto a lightly floured surface. Divide dough in half. Roll 1 portion into a 12-inch circle; spread with ¼ cup butter. Cut circle into 12 wedges. Roll up each wedge, beginning at wide end. Place on lightly greased large baking sheets, point sides down, leaving 2 inches of space between rolls; curve ends into a crescent shape. Repeat procedure using remaining dough and ¼ cup butter. Cover loosely, and let rise in a warm place, free from drafts, 30 minutes or until doubled in bulk.

Preheat oven to 400°. Bake rolls, uncovered, for 12 to 15 minutes or until lightly browned. Yield: 2 dozen.

Sister's Secret

For a tender, buttery crust, brush rolls or loaves with melted butter just before the final rising.

BUTTERSCOTCH ROLLS

(pictured on page 39)

Generously grease the pans for this recipe to keep the rolls from sticking.

1	package active dry yeast
1	cup warm milk (105° to 115°)
4½	cups all-purpose flour
½	cup sugar
1	teaspoon salt
¼	cup butter, melted
2	large eggs, lightly beaten
2	cups firmly packed brown sugar, divided
½	cup raisins
2	tablespoons ground cinnamon
2	cups coarsely chopped pecans
½	cup butter
½	cup butter, melted and divided

Combine yeast and warm milk in a 2-cup liquid measuring cup; let stand 5 minutes.

Combine flour, ½ cup sugar, and salt in a large bowl. Stir in yeast mixture, ¼ cup melted butter, and eggs. (Dough will be soft and sticky.)

Turn dough out onto a well-floured surface, and knead lightly 4 or 5 times. Place in a well-greased bowl, turning to grease top. Cover loosely, and let rise in a warm place (85°), free from drafts, 1 hour or until doubled in bulk.

Combine 1 cup brown sugar, raisins, and cinnamon in a small bowl. Set aside.

Combine remaining 1 cup brown sugar and pecans in a small bowl. Sprinkle pecan mixture evenly in bottoms of 2 well-greased 9-inch square or round pans. Dot pecan mixture with ½ cup butter. Set pans aside.

Punch dough down; turn out onto a well-floured surface. Divide dough in half. Roll 1 portion of dough into a 16- x 12-inch rectangle. Sprinkle half of raisin mixture evenly over dough.

Roll up dough jellyroll fashion, starting at the long side. Cut roll into 16 (1-inch) slices. Place slices, cut sides down, in a prepared pan, allowing ¼ inch of space between rolls; brush with ¼ cup melted butter. Repeat procedure with remaining dough, raisin mixture, and ¼ cup melted butter.

Cover loosely, and let rise in a warm place, free from drafts, 1 hour or until rolls rise to tops of pans.

Preheat oven to 375°. Bake rolls, uncovered, for 25 to 30 minutes or until lightly browned. Invert pans onto wax paper; let rolls stand, covered with pans, 1 minute. Remove pans, scraping any remaining pecan mixture from pan onto rolls. Serve warm. Yield: 32 rolls.

Sister's Secret

The oven is the perfect draft-free, temperature-controlled environment for letting dough rise. Place the dough on the middle rack of the oven and a pan of hot water on the bottom rack. Close the oven door, and allow the yeast to go to work.

SISTER'S STICKY BUNS

These rolls are so gooey and wonderful, they're worth every ounce of effort it takes to prepare them.

🐚 Small whole pecans are a pretty substitute for the coarsely chopped pecans.

1	cup water
½	cup sugar, divided
½	cup butter
1	package active dry yeast
½	cup warm water (105° to 115°)
1	teaspoon sugar
1	large egg, lightly beaten
4½	cups all-purpose flour, divided
1	teaspoon salt
1	cup butter, melted and divided
1½	cups firmly packed brown sugar, divided
½	cup light corn syrup
1½	cups coarsely chopped pecans
1	tablespoon ground cinnamon

Combine 1 cup water, ¼ cup sugar, and ½ cup butter in a saucepan; heat until butter melts, stirring occasionally. Cool to 105° to 115°.

Combine yeast, warm water, and 1 teaspoon sugar in a 1-cup liquid measuring cup; let stand 5 minutes. Combine butter mixture and yeast mixture. Add egg; stir well.

Combine yeast mixture, 2 cups flour, and salt in a large bowl. Add remaining 2½ cups flour, ½ cup at a time, stirring vigorously until dough is no longer sticky and pulls away from sides of bowl. Brush or lightly rub dough with some of the melted butter. Cover loosely, and let rise in a warm place (85°), free from drafts, 1 hour or until doubled in bulk.

Combine ½ cup melted butter, 1 cup brown sugar, corn syrup, and pecans; sprinkle mixture evenly in bottom of a well-greased 13- x 9- x 2-inch pan. Set pan aside. Combine remaining ½ cup brown sugar, remaining ¼ cup sugar, and cinnamon in a small bowl; set aside.

Punch dough down; turn out onto a well-floured surface. Roll dough into an 18- x 15-inch rectangle. Brush dough generously with some of the remaining melted butter; sprinkle evenly with cinnamon mixture. Roll up dough jellyroll fashion, starting at the long side. Cut roll into 12 (1½-inch) slices. Place slices, cut sides down, in prepared pan. Brush slices with remaining melted butter. Cover loosely, and let rise in a warm place, free from drafts, 1 hour or until tops of rolls rise just above top of pan.

Preheat oven to 350°. Bake rolls, uncovered, for 18 to 22 minutes or until golden. Cool in pan on a wire rack 8 minutes. Invert pan onto wax paper; let rolls stand, covered with pan, 1 minute. Remove pan, scraping any remaining pecan mixture from pan onto rolls. Serve warm. Yield: 1 dozen.

Sister's Secrets

Here are a few of my tried-and-true secrets
to help ensure success in making bread:

- *Preheat the oven before starting final preparation.*
  Then the oven is ready when you are.
- *Bake on the center rack of the oven unless the recipe*
  directs otherwise. Baking on the lowest rack
  or the highest rack could mean burned
  bread bottoms or tops.
- *Remove breads and rolls from the pans immediately*
  unless otherwise directed. Steam condensation
  can cause soggy crusts.

No-Knead Rolls

¾   cup water
¾   cup milk
⅓   cup butter
3⅓ cups all-purpose flour, divided
¼   cup sugar
1   package active dry yeast
1   large egg, lightly beaten
1   teaspoon salt
¼   cup butter, melted

Combine first 3 ingredients in a saucepan; heat until butter melts, stirring occasionally. Cool to 120° to 130°.

Combine 1½ cups flour, sugar, and yeast in a large bowl. Add butter mixture and egg to flour mixture; stir until well blended. Add remaining flour and salt, stirring until dough pulls away from sides of bowl. Brush or lightly rub dough with some of the melted butter. Cover loosely; let rise in a warm place (85°), free from drafts, 45 minutes or until doubled in bulk.

Stir dough several times. Spoon dough into greased muffin pans, filling two-thirds full. Brush or lightly rub rolls with remaining melted butter. Cover loosely, and let rise in a warm place, free from drafts, 30 minutes or until doubled in bulk.

Preheat oven to 400°. Bake rolls, uncovered, for 15 to 20 minutes or until lightly browned. Remove rolls from pans immediately. Yield: 18 rolls.

Butterscotch Rolls (page 34)

BISCUITS & SCONES

At our house, we never sat down to dinner without Mamie's Everyday Biscuits. I think we took them for granted, feeling that everyone must have been so blessed. Mamie's biscuits were small and flat, cut out with an old baking powder can. We used them as buttery little shovels to scoop up the field peas or bits of green tomato relish on our plates. Mama kept any leftover biscuits on a plate on top of the stove, and we'd race each other home after school to eat them. (But there were rarely enough left over for this treat.) Just thinking about those wonderful little biscuits takes me back to my childhood.

As for scones, I learned to appreciate them in my adult years. Scones are the first cousins of biscuits, but richer. They're usually baked in a round pan, cut into wedges, and served warm, accompanied by jam and butter.

Mystery Biscuits (page 48)

FOOLPROOF DINNER BISCUITS

These melt-in-your-mouth gems are so rich and flavorful that no one will believe how easy they are to make—unless you tell them!

❧ Don't be tempted to bake these biscuits in standard muffin pans. Foolproof Dinner Biscuits are so tender and delicate that they will fall apart if baked in pans larger than those called for in the recipe.

½   cup butter
½   cup margarine
2   cups self-rising flour
1   (8-ounce) carton sour cream

Preheat oven to 400°.

Cut butter and margarine into flour with a pastry blender until mixture is crumbly. Add sour cream, stirring with a fork just until dry ingredients are moistened. (Dough will be very soft and sticky.)

Spoon dough into greased miniature (1½-inch) muffin pans, filling two-thirds full. Bake for 20 minutes or until very lightly browned. Carefully remove from pans. Yield: 2 dozen.

DILLY DROP BISCUITS

Use the fresh dillweed growing in your summer garden to flavor these easy biscuits.

❧ Substitute 1 teaspoon dried dillweed for 1 tablespoon fresh, if desired. Fresh or dried basil or rosemary works well in this recipe, too.

2   cups all-purpose flour
1   teaspoon baking powder
½   teaspoon baking soda
½   teaspoon salt
1½   teaspoons sugar
1   tablespoon chopped fresh dillweed
2   tablespoons shortening
¾   cup buttermilk
     Grated Parmesan cheese

Preheat oven to 400°.

Combine first 6 ingredients in a large bowl. Cut in shortening with a pastry blender until mixture resembles coarse meal. Add buttermilk, stirring with a fork just until dry ingredients are moistened. (Dough will be very soft and sticky.)

Drop dough by spoonfuls onto a lightly greased large baking sheet; sprinkle lightly with Parmesan cheese. Bake for 12 to 15 minutes or until lightly browned. Yield: about 1½ dozen.

BUTTERMILK BISCUITS

2	cups all-purpose flour, sifted
2	teaspoons baking powder
½	teaspoon baking soda
½	teaspoon salt
½	cup butter
½	cup buttermilk

Preheat oven to 375°.

Combine first 4 ingredients in a large bowl; cut in butter with a pastry blender until mixture resembles coarse meal. Add buttermilk, stirring with a fork just until dry ingredients are moistened.

Turn dough out onto a lightly floured surface, and knead lightly 3 or 4 times. Roll or pat dough to ½-inch thickness; cut with a floured 2-inch biscuit cutter. Place biscuits on a lightly greased large baking sheet. Bake for 12 to 15 minutes or until golden. Yield: about 1½ dozen.

WHIPPED CREAM BISCUITS

You've probably seen recipes for whipping cream biscuits, but these actually use whipped cream as the liquid ingredient.

⤳ These tender biscuits require a gentle touch, from folding in the whipped cream to kneading and rolling out the dough.

2	cups all-purpose flour
1	tablespoon baking powder
¾	teaspoon salt
2	teaspoons sugar
1	cup whipping cream

Preheat oven to 425°.

Sift first 4 ingredients together into a large bowl.

Beat whipping cream with an electric mixer until stiff peaks form. Fold whipped cream into flour mixture just until dry ingredients are moistened.

Turn dough out onto a lightly floured surface, and knead lightly 1 minute or until dough is smooth and no longer sticky. Roll dough to ¼-inch thickness; cut with a floured 1½-inch biscuit cutter. Place biscuits on a lightly greased large baking sheet, leaving 1 inch of space between biscuits. Bake for 10 to 12 minutes or until golden. Yield: 2½ dozen.

Sister's Secret

Most biscuits and scones contain solid fat such as shortening or butter, which is cut into the dry ingredients with a pastry blender until the mixture resembles coarse meal. The tiny balls of solid fat created with the pastry blender melt into layers throughout the biscuits as they bake, forming those desirable fluffy layers.

MAMIE'S EVERYDAY BISCUITS

2	cups all-purpose flour
2	teaspoons baking powder
¾	teaspoon salt
¾	cup milk
¼	cup vegetable oil
½	cup all-purpose flour, divided
2	tablespoons vegetable oil

Preheat oven to 400°.

Combine first 3 ingredients in a large bowl. Combine milk and ¼ cup oil; add to flour mixture, stirring with a fork just until dry ingredients are moistened.

Sprinkle ¼ cup flour evenly over work surface; turn dough out onto floured surface. Sprinkle dough with remaining ¼ cup flour. Roll or pat dough to ¼-inch thickness; fold dough in half. Roll or pat entire surface one time only to set the dough for cutting. (Dough should be slightly less than ½-inch thick.) Cut biscuits with a floured 1½-inch biscuit cutter.

Pour 2 tablespoons oil into one end of a 15- x 10- x 1-inch jellyroll pan, tilting pan slightly to keep oil pooled. Dredge each biscuit generously on both sides in pooled oil; arrange in pan, leaving about 1 inch of space between biscuits. Wipe out any leftover oil with a paper towel. Bake for 15 to 20 minutes or until golden. Yield: about 1½ dozen.

Sister's Secret

Thoroughly mix baking powder into flour to keep biscuits from having a bitter taste.

QUICK BISCUITS

🐦 For fluffier biscuits, stir ½ teaspoon baking soda into ½ cup buttermilk, and substitute this mixture for the milk. For biscuits with crisp, golden outsides and tender, fluffy insides, use the cold mix straight from the refrigerator.

2   cups Refrigerator Biscuit Mix
½   cup milk

Preheat oven to 475°.

Combine Refrigerator Biscuit Mix and milk, stirring with a fork just until dry ingredients are moistened.

Turn dough out onto a lightly floured surface, and knead lightly 10 to 12 times or until dough is no longer sticky. Roll or pat dough to ½-inch thickness; cut with a floured 2-inch biscuit cutter. Place biscuits on a lightly greased large baking sheet, leaving 1 inch of space between biscuits. Bake for 8 to 10 minutes or until lightly browned. Yield: about 1 dozen.

REFRIGERATOR BISCUIT MIX

With this handy mix in your refrigerator, you'll never have to buy canned biscuits again.

8   cups all-purpose flour
3   tablespoons plus 1 teaspoon baking
          powder
2   teaspoons salt
2   tablespoons sugar
1½   cups shortening

Sift first 4 ingredients together into a large bowl. Cut in shortening with a pastry blender until mixture resembles coarse meal. Store flour mixture in a large airtight container in refrigerator up to 4 weeks. Yield: about 10 cups.

ANGEL BISCUITS

I have no less than five recipes for Angel Biscuits in my files, but my choice for the one to include in this book was easy—my great aunt Charlotte's recipe.

1	package active dry yeast
¼	cup warm water (105° to 115°)
¾	cup warm buttermilk (105° to 115°)
2½	cups all-purpose flour
½	teaspoon baking powder
½	teaspoon baking soda
½	teaspoon salt
2	tablespoons sugar
½	cup shortening

Combine yeast and warm water in a 2-cup liquid measuring cup; let stand 5 minutes. Add warm buttermilk; stir well.

Combine flour and next 4 ingredients in a large bowl; cut in shortening with a pastry blender until mixture resembles coarse meal. Add yeast mixture, stirring with a fork just until dry ingredients are moistened.

Turn dough out onto a lightly floured surface, and knead 10 to 15 times or until dough is smooth and no longer sticky. Roll dough to ¾-inch thickness; cut with a floured 2-inch biscuit cutter. Place biscuits on an ungreased large baking sheet, and cover with a towel. Let rise in a warm place (85°), free from drafts, 30 to 45 minutes or until doubled in bulk.

Preheat oven to 400°. Bake biscuits, uncovered, for 15 minutes or until golden. Yield: 1 dozen.

MYSTERY BISCUITS

(pictured on page 40)

You know these biscuits . . . you've eaten them at a well-known fast-food restaurant for years.

1	package active dry yeast
¼	cup warm water (105° to 115°)
6	cups self-rising flour, sifted and divided
1	cup shortening, melted and cooled to 105° to 115°
2	cups buttermilk
2	teaspoons sugar
1	teaspoon baking soda
	Melted butter

Combine yeast and warm water in a 1-cup liquid measuring cup; let stand 5 minutes.

Combine 1 cup flour and melted shortening in a large bowl; stir in yeast mixture.

Combine buttermilk, sugar, and soda. Gradually add remaining 5 cups flour to yeast mixture alternately with buttermilk mixture, stirring until mixture is well blended. Cover bowl tightly with plastic wrap; chill dough for 2 hours.

Preheat oven to 450°.

Turn dough out onto a well-floured surface, and knead lightly 3 or 4 times. Pat dough to ½-inch thickness; cut with a floured 3-inch biscuit cutter. Place biscuits on lightly greased large baking sheets, leaving 1 inch of space between biscuits. Bake for 8 to 10 minutes or until golden. Brush with melted butter. Yield: 15 biscuits.

Glazed Orange Scones

(pictured on page 2)

2	cups all-purpose flour
2	teaspoons baking powder
½	teaspoon baking soda
½	teaspoon salt
⅓	cup sugar
½	cup butter
⅓	cup milk
2	tablespoons plus ½ teaspoon grated orange rind, divided
⅓	cup plus 2 tablespoons orange juice, divided
½	cup sifted powdered sugar

Preheat oven to 375°.

Combine first 5 ingredients in a large bowl. Cut in butter with a pastry blender until mixture resembles coarse meal. Combine milk, 2 tablespoons orange rind, and ⅓ cup orange juice; add to flour mixture, stirring with a fork just until dry ingredients are moistened.

Drop dough by spoonfuls into 8 mounds on a lightly greased large baking sheet, leaving 1 inch of space between scones. Bake for 8 to 10 minutes or until golden. Transfer to a wire rack, and let cool.

Combine remaining ½ teaspoon orange rind, remaining 2 tablespoons orange juice, and powdered sugar; drizzle over cooled scones. Yield: 8 scones.

SISTER'S SCONES

I love to serve these pretty little scones at parties.

🌀 You may want to soak the raisins in brandy or sherry for one hour to plump them and give them extra flavor. Drain and stir the raisins into the flour mixture as directed.

4½	cups all-purpose flour
2	teaspoons baking powder
½	teaspoon baking soda
3	tablespoons sugar
1	cup butter
1	cup golden raisins
1	cup plus 3 tablespoons whipping cream, divided

Preheat oven to 375°.

Combine first 4 ingredients in a large bowl. Cut in butter with a pastry blender until mixture is crumbly. Stir in raisins. Add 1 cup whipping cream, stirring with a fork just until dry ingredients are moistened.

Turn dough out onto a lightly floured surface, and knead lightly 10 to 12 times or until smooth and no longer sticky. Roll or pat dough to ½-inch thickness; cut with a floured 1-inch scalloped cookie cutter. Place scones on lightly greased large baking sheets, leaving 1 inch of space between scones. Brush scones with remaining 3 tablespoons whipping cream. Bake for 15 to 20 minutes or until lightly browned. Yield: 40 scones.

APRICOT SCONES

These scones are made from a rich biscuit dough that contains eggs and fruit.

2	cups all-purpose flour
1	tablespoon baking powder
½	teaspoon salt
2	tablespoons sugar
½	cup butter
½	cup chopped dried apricots
2	large eggs, lightly beaten
½	cup milk

Preheat oven to 425°.

Combine first 4 ingredients in a large bowl. Cut in butter with a pastry blender until mixture resembles coarse meal. Stir in apricots.

Combine eggs and milk; reserve 2 tablespoons egg mixture. Add remaining egg mixture to flour mixture; stir with a fork just until dry ingredients are moistened.

Turn dough out onto a lightly floured surface, and knead lightly 8 to 10 times or until dough is smooth and no longer sticky. Place dough on a lightly greased large baking sheet, and pat into an 8-inch circle with floured hands. Cut dough into 8 wedges with a floured sharp knife. (Do not separate wedges.) Brush dough with reserved egg mixture. Bake for 12 to 15 minutes or until golden. Yield: 8 scones.

Cutting the dough into wedges but not separating them helps create the scones' distinctive pie shape and soft sides.

DEVONSHIRE SCONES

This traditional English scone is a specialty of the Devonshire area.

1½	cups all-purpose flour
2	teaspoons baking powder
½	teaspoon salt
¾	cup rolled oats
¼	cup firmly packed brown sugar
1	teaspoon ground cinnamon
½	cup butter
½	cup milk
2	tablespoons butter, melted

Preheat oven to 375°.

Combine first 6 ingredients in a large bowl. Cut in ½ cup butter with a pastry blender until mixture resembles coarse meal. Add milk, stirring with a fork just until dry ingredients are moistened.

Turn dough out onto a lightly floured surface, and knead lightly 3 or 4 times. Place dough on a lightly greased large baking sheet, and pat into a 6-inch circle with floured hands. Cut dough into 8 wedges with a floured sharp knife. (Do not separate wedges.) Brush dough with melted butter. Bake for 20 to 25 minutes or until golden. Yield: 8 scones.

Sister's Secret

After adding the liquid ingredients to the flour mixture for scones and biscuits, stir with a fork only until the dry ingredients are moistened. Too much stirring creates a heavy, dense bread.

MUFFINS & BREAKFAST BREADS

I love to bake early in the morning, filling the house with the wonderful aroma of fresh-baked breakfast breads before the rest of the family stirs. There's something about breakfast breads—muffins, French toast, pancakes, waffles—that brings back memories of family vacations. We loved eating breakfast on vacation, eagerly ordering those quick breads that could easily be prepared at home but that somehow tasted especially good while on vacation.

Try your hand at some of my favorites such as Lemon-Blueberry Muffins, Fly-off-the-Plate Pancakes, French Toast with a Twist, and Three-Egg Waffles.

APPLESAUCE MUFFINS

1   cup butter, softened
2   cups sugar
2   large eggs
1   teaspoon vanilla extract
4   cups all-purpose flour
1   teaspoon ground cinnamon
½   teaspoon ground allspice
½   teaspoon ground cloves
¾   cup chopped pecans
1   (16-ounce) jar applesauce
2   teaspoons baking soda

Preheat oven to 400°.

Beat butter at medium speed of an electric mixer until creamy. Add sugar, beating well. Add eggs and vanilla; beat well. Set mixture aside.

Sift flour and next 3 ingredients together; stir in pecans.

Combine applesauce and soda, stirring until mixture is foamy; add to butter mixture alternately with flour mixture, beginning and ending with flour mixture. Beat at low speed just until blended after each addition.

Spoon batter into greased muffin pans, filling two-thirds full. Bake for 12 to 15 minutes or until muffins are golden. Remove from pans immediately. Yield: 2 dozen.

MUFFINS TROPICALE

(pictured on page 2)

2 cups all-purpose flour
2 teaspoons baking powder
½ teaspoon baking soda
½ teaspoon salt
½ cup firmly packed light brown sugar
2 tablespoons sugar
1 large egg, lightly beaten
1 (8-ounce) can crushed pineapple
1 cup sour cream
½ cup chopped macadamia nuts
⅓ cup vegetable oil

Preheat oven to 400°.

Combine first 6 ingredients in a large bowl; make a well in center of mixture. Combine egg and remaining 4 ingredients; add to flour mixture, stirring just until dry ingredients are moistened.

Spoon batter into greased muffin pans, filling two-thirds full. Bake for 20 to 24 minutes or until muffins are golden. Remove from pans immediately. Yield: 1½ dozen.

Sister's Secret

For easy cleanup, use paper baking cups to line muffin pans. Spray the insides of the paper cups with vegetable cooking spray, and you'll be able to easily peel the cups off the muffins.

LEMON–BLUEBERRY MUFFINS

Use the large eyes of the grater to grate lemon rind unless otherwise directed. The larger pieces of rind will add more lemon flavor to the muffins.

2¼	cups all-purpose flour, divided
⅓	cup firmly packed brown sugar
2	tablespoons butter
1	cup fresh or frozen blueberries
2	tablespoons sugar (optional)
	Coarsely grated rind of 2 medium lemons
1	teaspoon sugar
½	cup butter, softened
½	cup plus 2 tablespoons sugar
2	large eggs
½	teaspoon baking powder
½	teaspoon salt
½	teaspoon baking soda
1	cup buttermilk

Preheat oven to 400°. Combine ¼ cup flour and brown sugar; cut in 2 tablespoons butter with a pastry blender until mixture resembles coarse crumbs. Set aside. Toss berries with 2 tablespoons sugar, if desired; set aside. Combine lemon rind and 1 teaspoon sugar; set aside.

Beat softened butter with an electric mixer until creamy. Add ½ cup plus 2 tablespoons sugar; beat well. Add eggs; beat well. Combine remaining 2 cups flour, baking powder, and salt. Combine soda and buttermilk; add to butter mixture alternately with flour mixture, beginning and ending with flour mixture. Beat at low speed just until blended. Fold in berries and rind.

Spoon batter into greased muffin pans, filling three-fourths full. Sprinkle brown sugar mixture evenly over batter. Bake for 15 to 18 minutes or until golden. Let stand 5 minutes in pans. Remove from pans. Yield: 1½ dozen.

Lemon-Blueberry Muffins

ORANGE BLOSSOM MUFFINS

1	cup butter, softened
¼	cup orange marmalade
1	large orange
½	cup butter, melted
1	large egg, lightly beaten
2	cups all-purpose flour
1	teaspoon baking powder
1	teaspoon baking soda
½	teaspoon salt
¾	cup sugar

Preheat oven to 400°.

Beat softened butter at medium speed of an electric mixer until creamy. Add marmalade; beat just until blended. Cover and chill marmalade mixture until ready to serve with muffins.

Coarsely grate orange rind. Remove white pith and seeds from orange; discard. Using kitchen shears, finely chop orange into a bowl; stir in grated rind, melted butter, and egg.

Combine flour and remaining 4 ingredients in a large bowl; make a well in center of mixture. Add orange mixture to flour mixture, stirring just until dry ingredients are moistened.

Spoon batter into greased muffin pans, filling two-thirds full. Bake for 15 to 20 minutes or until muffins are golden. Remove from pans immediately. Serve muffins warm with marmalade mixture. Yield: 1 dozen.

Three-Egg Waffles (page 66)

SWEET POTATO MUFFINS

This is a wonderful way to use leftover sweet potatoes. I bake these muffins to accompany after–Thanksgiving meals.

One large sweet potato, cooked and mashed, will give you the amount you need for this recipe.

¼	cup butter, softened
½	cup sugar
⅔	cup cooked, mashed sweet potato
1	large egg
¾	cup all-purpose flour
½	teaspoon salt
½	teaspoon ground cinnamon
¼	teaspoon ground nutmeg
½	cup chopped pecans or walnuts
¼	cup raisins, chopped
½	cup milk

Preheat oven to 400°.

Beat butter at medium speed of an electric mixer until creamy; add sugar, beating well. Add sweet potato and egg; beat well.

Combine flour and next 3 ingredients. Stir in pecans and raisins. Add flour mixture to butter mixture alternately with milk, beginning and ending with flour mixture. Beat just until blended after each addition.

Spoon batter into greased muffin pans, filling two-thirds full. Bake for 20 to 25 minutes or until a wooden pick inserted in center of a muffin comes out clean. Remove from pans immediately. Yield: 1 dozen.

SURPRISE MUFFINS

The surprise in these tender, sweet muffins is the jalapeño bite and cheesy flavor.

2	cups all-purpose flour
1	tablespoon baking powder
½	teaspoon salt
¾	cup sugar
1	large egg, lightly beaten
¾	cup milk
⅓	cup vegetable oil
1	cup (4 ounces) shredded sharp Cheddar cheese
2	to 3 tablespoons diced pickled jalapeño pepper

Preheat oven to 400°.

Combine first 4 ingredients in a large bowl; make a well in center of mixture. Combine egg, milk, and oil; add to flour mixture, stirring just until dry ingredients are moistened. Fold in cheese and pepper.

Spoon batter into greased muffin pans, filling two-thirds full. Bake for 20 to 25 minutes or until muffins are golden. Remove from pans immediately. Yield: 1 dozen.

Sister's Secret

Stir muffin batter just until the dry ingredients are moistened. Overstirring will cause muffins to peak and to have tunnels and a coarse texture.

EASY ENGLISH MUFFINS

3	cups all-purpose flour
1½	teaspoons baking powder
1	teaspoon salt
¼	teaspoon baking soda
2	tablespoons sugar
1	large egg, lightly beaten
⅔	cup buttermilk
2	tablespoons butter, melted
	White cornmeal (optional)

Combine first 5 ingredients in a large bowl; make a well in center of mixture. Combine egg, buttermilk, and butter; add to dry ingredients. Stir with a wooden spoon 3 minutes or until dough is no longer sticky.

Turn dough out onto a well-floured surface; roll out to ¼- to ⅜-inch thickness. Cut out dough using a floured 3-inch biscuit cutter. Reroll and cut until all dough is used. Dust muffins with cornmeal for crunchy texture, if desired.

Heat griddle to medium (350°). Place muffins on ungreased griddle, and bake until muffins are puffed and crusts are light golden (about 4 to 5 minutes on each side). Remove from griddle, and let cool on wire racks. Split in half, and toast before serving. Yield: 16 muffins.

BREAKFAST PUFF

1	large egg, separated
1	tablespoon sugar
1	tablespoon butter, melted
2	cups all-purpose flour
2½	teaspoons baking powder
1	cup milk
	Sifted powdered sugar

Preheat oven to 450°.

Beat egg yolk in a mixing bowl at medium speed of an electric mixer until thick and pale. Add 1 tablespoon sugar and butter; beat well.

Combine flour and baking powder. Add flour mixture to egg yolk mixture alternately with milk, beginning and ending with flour mixture. Beat just until blended after each addition. Beat egg white until stiff peaks form; fold beaten white into batter.

Pour batter into a greased and floured 13- x 9- x 2-inch pan. Bake for 20 minutes or until puffy and golden. Sprinkle with powdered sugar. Serve hot with butter and honey or syrup, if desired. Yield: 6 servings.

FRENCH TOAST WITH A TWIST

Day-old French bread works best for this unique French toast. What's the twist? The bread is coated in a beaten egg white batter and deep-fried until puffy and golden.

⅔	**cup milk**
2	**tablespoons sugar**
¼	**teaspoon ground nutmeg**
2	**large eggs, separated**
	Vegetable oil
6	**(¾-inch-thick) slices French bread**
	Sifted powdered sugar

Combine first 3 ingredients in a shallow dish; set aside.

Beat egg whites at high speed of an electric mixer until stiff peaks form; add yolks, beating at low speed just until blended.

Pour oil to depth of ½ inch into a large heavy skillet; place over medium-high heat. Dredge bread in milk mixture, and then dip in egg mixture. Fry bread in hot oil until golden on both sides, about 3 minutes. Drain bread on paper towels. Sprinkle with powdered sugar. Serve warm with syrup, if desired. Yield: 3 servings.

Fly-off-the-Plate Pancakes

These tender, light-as-a-feather pancakes were my grandmother Wood's favorite.

1	cup all-purpose flour
1	tablespoon baking powder
1	tablespoon sugar
¼	teaspoon salt
1	large egg, lightly beaten
1	cup milk
2½	tablespoons sour cream
2	tablespoons butter, melted
	Vegetable oil

For thin pancakes, stir a little extra milk into the batter. If you prefer thick pancakes, reduce the amount of milk called for in the recipe ingredients.

Combine first 4 ingredients in a large bowl. Combine egg and next 3 ingredients, stirring with a wire whisk until frothy; add to dry ingredients, stirring just until smooth.

Heat a large griddle or skillet to medium-high (375°). Lightly grease cooking surface with oil or coat with vegetable cooking spray. For each pancake, pour ¼ cup batter onto hot surface. Cook pancakes until tops are covered with bubbles and edges look cooked; turn and cook other side. Serve warm with butter and syrup or honey, if desired. Yield: about 1 dozen.

Sister's Secret

The cooking surface for pancakes should not be greasy. Apply a little oil between batches, and lightly wipe it off with a paper towel. Or lightly coat the cooking surface with vegetable cooking spray between batches.

THREE-EGG WAFFLES

(pictured on page 58)

2	cups all-purpose flour
1	tablespoon baking powder
½	teaspoon salt
3	large eggs, separated
1	cup milk
¼	cup vegetable oil
	Sliced fresh strawberries
	Sifted powdered sugar
	Garnishes: fresh mint sprigs, pansies

Combine first 3 ingredients in a large mixing bowl. Beat egg yolks at medium speed of an electric mixer until thick and pale. Add milk and oil; beat well. Add egg mixture to flour mixture, beating at low speed just until mixture is smooth.

Beat egg whites at high speed of mixer until stiff peaks form; gently fold beaten whites into batter.

Pour amount of batter recommended in manufacturer's instructions onto a preheated, oiled waffle iron; spread batter to edges. Bake until steaming stops and waffle is lightly browned. Top with sliced strawberries, and sprinkle with sifted powdered sugar. Garnish, if desired. Serve warm with butter and syrup or honey. Yield: 10 (4-inch) waffles.

Sister's Secret

Waffles tend to stick to the cooking surface if it isn't well greased. Either coat the surface with vegetable cooking spray, or brush lightly with vegetable oil.

CORNBREADS

*I*f biscuits are the heart of Southern bread baking, then cornbread is surely the soul. You simply can't have a Southern-style meal without it—or at least my family believed this. In addition to biscuits, Daddy liked to have Authentic Old-South Cornbread Patties for dinner. Mamie used both white and yellow cornmeal, which she simply referred to as "meal," and her cornbread basically consisted of cornmeal, water, and salt, the same combination that generations of good cooks before her had used. At our table, this fried cornbread was often served with turnip greens.

It was not until I was grown that I developed a taste for some of the old-time, traditional cornbreads you will find in this chapter—soufflé-textured Spoonbread; my own rich Southern Cornbread; and a real favorite, yeasty and light Angel Corn Sticks. When you try these recipes, I hope that you discover that cornbread truly is food for the soul and a Southern delight.

SISTER'S SOUTHERN CORNBREAD

(pictured on page 76)

True Southern cornbread is made with white cornmeal, but you can substitute yellow cornmeal.

⌇ You can bake this recipe in muffin pans, corn stick pans, or your grand-mother's cast-iron skillet, if you prefer.

¾	cup butter, melted and divided
1	cup sour cream
¾	cup buttermilk
2	tablespoons water
2	large eggs, lightly beaten
1½	cups self-rising white cornmeal

Preheat oven to 400°. Grease bottom of a 9-inch round cakepan with 1 tablespoon melted butter; set aside.

Combine remaining melted butter, sour cream, and next 3 ingredients; add cornmeal, stirring until moistened.

Pour batter into prepared pan. Bake for 35 to 40 minutes or until golden. Yield: 8 servings.

Corn Muffins: Grease muffin pans with 1 tablespoon melted butter. Prepare batter as directed; pour into prepared pans, filling two-thirds full. Bake at 400° for 18 to 20 minutes or until muffins are golden. Remove muffins from pans imme-diately. Yield: 1 dozen.

Sister's Secret

Perfect cornbread batter should be thin enough to pour and should not show the tracks of the spoon when you stir it. If the batter is too thick, just stir in additional buttermilk or milk.

SISTER'S JALAPEÑO CORNBREAD

(pictured on page 76 and on back cover)

I've suggested a range for the number of fresh jalapeño peppers to use in this recipe. Add at your own risk!

¾	cup butter, melted and divided
1	cup canned white cream-style corn
1	cup sour cream
2	large eggs, lightly beaten
1½	cups self-rising cornmeal
1	cup (4 ounces) shredded sharp Cheddar cheese
2	to 4 fresh jalapeño peppers, seeded and chopped

To protect your skin and eyes, wear rubber gloves when seeding and chopping fresh jalapeño peppers. The seeds and veins contain oils that will cause your skin to tingle and your eyes to burn.

Preheat oven to 400°. Grease bottom of a 9-inch round cakepan with 1 tablespoon melted butter; set aside.

Combine remaining melted butter, corn, sour cream, and eggs in a large bowl; add cornmeal, stirring until moistened. Stir in cheese and chopped pepper.

Pour batter into prepared pan. Bake for 35 to 40 minutes or until golden. Yield: 8 servings.

Corn Muffins: Grease muffin pans with 1 tablespoon melted butter. Prepare batter as directed; pour into prepared pans, filling two-thirds full. Bake at 400° for 18 to 20 minutes or until muffins are golden. Remove muffins from pans immediately. Yield: 1 dozen.

Broccoli Cornbread

4   large eggs, lightly beaten
1   (10-ounce) package frozen chopped
        broccoli, thawed
1   small onion, finely chopped
1   green onion, finely chopped
1   cup small-curd cottage cheese
½   cup butter, melted
1½   cups self-rising cornmeal
1   teaspoon sugar

Preheat oven to 350°.

Combine first 6 ingredients in a large bowl; add cornmeal and sugar, stirring until dry ingredients are moistened.

Pour batter into a lightly greased 13- x 9- x 2-inch baking dish. Bake for 40 to 45 minutes or until cornbread is golden. Yield: 12 to 15 servings.

Sister's Secret

Substitute plain cornmeal for self-rising using the following formula: For each cup of self-rising cornmeal called for, substitute 1 cup plain cornmeal combined with 1½ teaspoons baking powder and ½ teaspoon salt.

CORNBREAD SKILLET SUPPER

This skillet supper, served with salsa and cowboy beans, is a favorite football game feast at my house.

1	pound ground chuck
2	medium onions, coarsely chopped
1	medium-size green pepper, coarsely chopped
1	teaspoon salt
¼	teaspoon pepper
1	cup plain cornmeal
1	teaspoon salt
½	teaspoon baking soda
1	cup milk
¼	cup bacon drippings
2	large eggs, lightly beaten
1	(15-ounce) can cream-style corn
2	cups (8 ounces) shredded Cheddar cheese, divided

Preheat oven to 350°.

Cook first 3 ingredients in a large skillet over medium-high heat until meat is browned, stirring until it crumbles. Drain; return to skillet. Stir in 1 teaspoon salt and ¼ teaspoon pepper. Set aside.

Place a well-greased 10-inch cast-iron skillet in oven for 5 to 7 minutes or until hot.

Combine cornmeal and next 6 ingredients in a large bowl, stirring until dry ingredients are moistened. Pour half of cornmeal mixture into hot skillet; sprinkle with 1 cup cheese and all of meat mixture. Pour remaining cornmeal mixture over meat mixture; sprinkle with remaining cheese. Bake for 45 to 55 minutes or until golden. Let stand 5 minutes before serving. Cut into wedges to serve. Yield: 6 to 8 servings.

Mamie's Cornbread Dressing

Canned chicken broth may be substituted for homemade turkey or chicken stock.

2   stalks celery, finely chopped
½   cup finely chopped green pepper
½   cup finely chopped onion
¼   cup butter, melted
1   recipe Sister's Southern Cornbread
       (page 68)
2   large eggs, lightly beaten
1   cup turkey or chicken stock
½   teaspoon salt
½   teaspoon ground sage
½   teaspoon ground thyme
½   teaspoon ground pepper

Preheat oven to 350°.

Cook first 3 ingredients in butter in a medium skillet over medium-high heat, stirring constantly, until tender. Spoon vegetable mixture into a large bowl. Crumble cornbread into bowl. Add eggs and remaining ingredients, stirring until well blended.

Spoon cornbread mixture evenly into a lightly greased 13- x 9- x 2-inch pan. Bake for 45 to 55 minutes or until golden and a wooden pick inserted in center comes out clean. Yield: 8 to 10 servings.

SISTER'S SPOONBREAD

Spoonbread, a Virginia specialty traditionally served with Smithfield ham, has the moist, spoonable texture of a soufflé.

3½	cups milk
1	cup plain white cornmeal, sifted
1	teaspoon salt
1	teaspoon sugar
2	tablespoons butter
4	large eggs, separated

Preheat oven to 350°.

Heat milk in a large saucepan over medium heat until hot, stirring often. (Do not boil.) Add cornmeal, salt, and sugar; cook, stirring constantly, until mixture comes to a boil. Cook, stirring constantly, 3 minutes. Remove pan from heat; stir in butter. Set aside, and let cool to touch. (Mixture does not have to cool completely.)

Beat egg yolks until thick and pale; add to cornmeal mixture, stirring until well blended. Beat egg whites at high speed of an electric mixer until stiff peaks form; fold into cornmeal mixture.

Pour batter into a greased 9-inch square pan. Bake for 50 to 60 minutes or until puffed and golden. Serve immediately. Yield: 6 to 8 servings.

COUNTRY CORN MUFFINS

1¼	cups plain cornmeal
¾	cup all-purpose flour
1	tablespoon plus 1 teaspoon baking powder
¾	teaspoon salt
1	tablespoon sugar
2	large eggs, lightly beaten
1	cup milk
¼	cup vegetable oil

Combine first 5 ingredients in a large bowl. Combine eggs, milk, and oil; add to cornmeal mixture, stirring until dry ingredients are moistened.

If using cast-iron muffin pans, place well-greased pans in a 425° oven for 5 minutes or until hot. Spoon batter into hot pans, filling two-thirds full. For regular muffin pans, spoon batter into greased pans, filling two-thirds full.

Bake at 425° for 12 to 15 minutes or until muffins are golden. Remove from pans immediately. Yield: 1 dozen.

Sister's Secret

Fill any empty muffin cups half full of water before baking to help distribute the heat evenly and to keep the muffins from overbrowning.

Country Corn Muffins (above), Angel Corn Sticks (page 77)

ANGEL CORN STICKS

(pictured on page 75)

The addition of yeast makes these corn sticks so light that you'll agree they're heavenly.

1	package active dry yeast
2	cups warm buttermilk (105° to 115°)
½	cup shortening, melted and cooled to 105° to 115°
1½	cups plain cornmeal
1	cup all-purpose flour
1½	teaspoons baking powder
1	teaspoon salt
½	teaspoon baking soda
1	tablespoon sugar
2	large eggs, lightly beaten
½	cup shortening, melted

Combine first 3 ingredients in a small bowl; let stand 5 minutes.

Combine cornmeal and next 5 ingredients in a large bowl. Add yeast mixture and eggs, stirring until well blended. Let batter stand 30 minutes. (Do not stir.)

Grease corn stick pans by spreading 1 teaspoon melted shortening evenly over surface of each mold. Heat corn stick pans in a 450° oven for 5 minutes or until oil sizzles.

Spoon batter into preheated molds, filling each half full. Bake at 450° for 12 to 15 minutes or until corn sticks are puffy and golden. Remove corn sticks from pans immediately. Serve warm. Yield: 2 dozen.

Front to back: *Sister's Jalapeño Cornbread (page 69), Sister's Southern Cornbread (page 68)*

HOE CAKES

Hoe cakes originated in the cotton fields of the antebellum South. Resourceful cooks heated a clean hoe in the fire, dropped a mound of cornmeal batter onto the blade, and propped the hoe up next to the fire to bake the cornbread. You're welcome to try this cooking method, but I think you'll enjoy hoe cakes hot off the griddle just as much.

🌿 Be careful not to cook the hoe cakes too fast. Reduce the heat as necessary while the cakes cook to prevent burning.

1½	cups plain cornmeal
1	teaspoon salt
1	teaspoon sugar
1½	tablespoons bacon drippings or melted butter
½	cup boiling water
½	cup ice water
	Vegetable oil

Combine first 5 ingredients, stirring until well blended. Stir in ice water.

Heat a cast-iron griddle or skillet over medium heat. When a drop of water dances and pops on the surface, brush the cooking surface with oil.

Drop batter by tablespoonfuls onto hot cooking surface; cook 3 to 4 minutes on each side or until cakes are lightly browned. Yield: 8 servings.

AUTHENTIC OLD-SOUTH CORNBREAD PATTIES

These patties are Daddy's favorite—especially when served with turnip greens. Every now and then, he adds a tablespoon of grated onion to the batter for a flavorful change.

2	cups plain white cornmeal
1	teaspoon baking powder
1	teaspoon salt
2½	cups hot water
¼	cup shortening

Combine first 3 ingredients in a large bowl. Add hot water, stirring until well blended.

Place shortening in a medium-size heavy skillet; heat over medium-high heat until a drop of water dances and pops on the surface. Spoon half of cornmeal mixture into skillet by tablespoonfuls; fry about 4 minutes on each side or until golden and crispy. Remove patties from skillet, and drain on paper towels. Reduce heat to medium, and repeat procedure using remaining half of cornmeal mixture. Serve hot. Yield: 1 dozen.

The consistency of the batter should be similar to that of the wet sand children use to make great sand castles at the beach.

Hush Puppies

Hush puppies supposedly got their name from the balls of fried cornbread that hunters tossed to their barking hounds while saying, "Hush puppy!"

	Vegetable oil
2	cups plain cornmeal
2	tablespoons all-purpose flour
1	tablespoon baking powder
2	teaspoons baking soda
1	teaspoon salt
1	large egg, lightly beaten
2	cups buttermilk
⅓	cup finely chopped sweet onion
	Ground red pepper to taste

Pour oil to depth of 3 inches into a deep-fat fryer or Dutch oven; heat to 375°.

Combine cornmeal and next 4 ingredients in a large bowl. Combine egg and remaining 3 ingredients; add to cornmeal mixture, stirring until dry ingredients are moistened.

Carefully drop batter by rounded teaspoonfuls into hot oil; fry hush puppies, a few at a time, 3 to 4 minutes or until golden, turning once. Drain on paper towels. Serve warm. Yield: about 2½ dozen.

Sister's Secret

To make hush puppy batter slide easily off the spoon into the hot oil, dip the spoon in ice water before scooping up the batter. This trick works well with any thick cornmeal batter.

HOLIDAY BREADS

It's the holidays—time for family and friends to gather and celebrate shared traditions. And in my family, these celebrations have always included some sort of homemade bread, whether it was slightly sweet Hot Cross Buns, a fruit-laden Yule Stollen, or even my Parkerhouse rolls. In fact, my bakery came about because so many folks wanted to serve my rolls during the Christmas holidays.

During those early years, the whole family pitched in to help me get the rolls out; even my youngest daughter could make them from memory. Funny thing, after making all those thousands of rolls, we still enjoy eating them at our family holiday dinners.

To make homemade bread a part of your holiday menu this year, try your hand at Holiday Strudel, Almond Christmas Braid, Easter Bread, or Challah. And don't forget that homemade breads are perfect gifts.

Holiday Strudel

(pictured on page 93)

Not only will your family enjoy this holiday breakfast favorite, but it makes a great gift for anyone on your list who has a sweet tooth.

If you would like to prepare only two strudels at a time, tightly wrap and chill the remaining portions of dough up to two days. The baked strudels freeze well for one month; just wrap them tightly. Thaw them at room temperature before serving.

1	cup butter, softened
½	(8-ounce) package cream cheese, softened
1	cup sour cream
5	cups all-purpose flour
2	(13-ounce) jars cherry preserves, divided
2	cups powdered sugar, sifted
¼	cup milk
½	teaspoon vanilla extract
1	cup sliced natural almonds, toasted
1	cup green candied cherries, quartered
1	cup red candied cherries, quartered

Beat butter and cream cheese at medium speed of an electric mixer until creamy. Add sour cream, beating until well blended. Add flour, 1 cup at a time, beating until dough pulls away from sides of bowl. Cover bowl tightly with plastic wrap, and chill at least 2 hours and up to 8 hours.

Preheat oven to 350°. Turn dough out onto a floured surface; divide into 4 equal portions. Prepare one strudel at a time; keep remaining dough wrapped and chilled until ready to use.

For each strudel, roll one portion of dough into a 16- x 12-inch rectangle. Spread one-fourth of preserves to within 1 inch of edges. Fold long sides of dough to meet in center, pressing edges to seal. Fold short sides of dough to meet in center, pressing edges to seal. Place strudel, seam side down, on one half of a large greased baking sheet. (You will be placing 2 strudels on each baking sheet.) Score strudel crosswise at 1-inch intervals using a sharp knife, cutting through top layer of dough to reveal preserves.

Bake at 350° for 45 minutes or until filling is bubbly. Remove strudels from baking sheets, and let cool on wire racks.

Place wax paper under wire racks. Combine powdered sugar, milk, and vanilla; stir until smooth. Drizzle mixture over strudels. Decorate immediately with almonds and candied cherries. Cut into slices to serve. Yield: 4 strudels.

TIPSY EGGNOG BREAD

2½	cups all-purpose flour
2	teaspoons baking powder
1	teaspoon salt
¼	teaspoon ground nutmeg
¼	teaspoon ground cinnamon
2	large eggs
1¼	cups eggnog
1	cup sugar
½	cup butter, melted
2	teaspoons bourbon
1	teaspoon vanilla extract

If you don't plan to enjoy this bread right away, wrap the cooled loaf in plastic wrap, and refrigerate up to two days.

Preheat oven to 350°. Grease the bottom only of a 9- x 5- x 3-inch loafpan. Set prepared pan aside.

Sift first 5 ingredients together. Set aside. Beat eggs in a large mixing bowl at high speed of an electric mixer until light and frothy. Add eggnog and remaining 4 ingredients, beating at medium speed until well blended.

Add flour mixture to eggnog mixture, ½ cup at a time, stirring just until dry ingredients are moistened after each addition.

Pour batter into prepared pan. Bake for 45 to 50 minutes or until a wooden pick inserted in center comes out clean. Cool loaf in pan on a wire rack 10 minutes; remove from pan, and let cool completely on a wire rack. Yield: 1 loaf.

CRANBERRY BREAD

Cranberry Bread makes a thoughtful hostess gift for the holidays.

Tightly wrap the cooled loaf in plastic wrap, and freeze up to one month.

1	cup fresh cranberries, coarsely chopped
1⅓	cups sugar
1	large orange
2	tablespoons butter, melted
	About ½ cup boiling water
1	large egg, lightly beaten
2	cups all-purpose flour
1½	teaspoons baking powder
½	teaspoon baking soda
½	teaspoon salt
1	cup chopped pecans

Preheat oven to 350°. Grease and flour a 9- x 5- x 3-inch loaf-pan. Set prepared pan aside.

Combine chopped cranberries and sugar in a medium bowl. Grate rind from orange using large eyes of a grater. Cut orange in half, and extract juice. Combine grated rind, juice, and melted butter in a 1-cup liquid measuring cup; add enough boiling water to orange juice mixture to equal 1 cup. Add orange juice mixture to cranberry mixture; let cool slightly. Stir in egg.

Combine flour and next 3 ingredients in a large bowl. Add cranberry mixture, stirring just until dry ingredients are moistened. Fold in pecans.

Pour batter into prepared pan. Bake for 1 hour or until a wooden pick inserted in center of loaf comes out clean. Cool in pan on a wire rack 10 minutes. Turn out onto a wire rack, and let cool completely. Yield: 1 loaf.

ALMOND CHRISTMAS BRAID

1   package active dry yeast
⅔   cup warm milk (105° to 115°)
2   tablespoons sugar
¼   cup butter, melted and divided
1   large egg, lightly beaten
2¼ cups all-purpose flour
1   tablespoon grated orange rind
½   teaspoon salt
1   cup powdered sugar, sifted
2   tablespoons milk
¼   teaspoon almond extract
½   cup blanched slivered almonds, toasted
    Red and green candied cherries (optional)

Combine yeast and warm milk in a 2-cup liquid measuring cup; let stand 5 minutes. Stir in 2 tablespoons sugar, 2 tablespoons melted butter, and egg. Combine flour, orange rind, and salt in a large bowl. Add yeast mixture; stir well.

Turn dough out onto a well-floured surface; knead until smooth and elastic (7 to 9 minutes). Place in a well-greased bowl, turning to grease top. Cover loosely; let rise in a warm place (85°), free from drafts, 1 hour or until doubled in bulk.

Punch down dough; turn out onto a lightly floured surface. Divide into thirds. Roll each third into a 24-inch rope. Place ropes on a large greased baking sheet. Braid ropes; join ends of ropes, and shape braid into an oval. Brush loaf with remaining melted butter. Cover loosely; let rise in a warm place, free from drafts, 45 minutes or until doubled in bulk.

Preheat oven to 350°. Bake for 30 to 40 minutes or until golden. Remove from baking sheet, and let cool on a wire rack.

Transfer braid to a large platter. Combine powdered sugar, 2 tablespoons milk, and almond extract; drizzle over braid. Sprinkle evenly with almonds. Decorate with candied cherries, if desired. Yield: 1 loaf.

THREE KINGS COFFEE RING

Follow tradition with this recipe's hidden gifts from the kings. Insert three small items into the bottom of the cooled cake before you decorate it. Surprise adults with silver charms or gold coins; delight children with plastic toys.

1	cup milk
½	cup sugar
¼	cup butter
1	package active dry yeast
3	cups all-purpose flour, divided
1	teaspoon salt
½	teaspoon ground cinnamon
2	large eggs
½	cup pecans, coarsely chopped
½	cup candied cherries and pineapple, chopped
1	tablespoon grated orange rind
1	teaspoon grated lemon rind
¼	cup butter, melted
1	cup powdered sugar, sifted
2	teaspoons orange juice
1	teaspoon half-and-half
	Red and green candied cherries (optional)
	Pecan halves (optional)

Combine first 3 ingredients in a saucepan; heat until butter melts, stirring occasionally. Cool to 105° to 115°. Add yeast; stir until dissolved. Let stand 5 minutes.

Combine 2 cups flour, salt, and cinnamon in a large mixing bowl. Gradually add yeast mixture, beating at low speed of an electric mixer until blended. Add eggs, one at a time, beating at medium speed just until blended after each addition. Beat 3 additional minutes at high speed. Add chopped pecans and next three ingredients; beat well. Stir in remaining 1 cup flour.

Turn dough out onto a well-floured surface, and knead until smooth and elastic (5 to 7 minutes). Place dough in a well-greased bowl, turning to grease top. Cover loosely, and let rise in a warm place (85°), free from drafts, 1 hour or until doubled in bulk.

Punch dough down; turn out onto a lightly floured surface. Roll dough into a rope approximately 24 inches long. Place rope of dough on a large greased baking sheet, and join ends together to form a ring, pressing to seal. Brush dough with melted butter. Cover loosely, and let rise in a warm place, free from drafts, 45 minutes or until doubled in bulk.

Preheat oven to 375°. Bake, uncovered, on center rack of oven for 10 minutes. Cover with aluminum foil, and bake 10 to 15 additional minutes until golden. Remove from baking sheet, and let cool on a wire rack.

Combine powdered sugar, orange juice, and half-and-half, stirring vigorously to form a somewhat stiff icing. (If icing seems too thin, add more powdered sugar.) Transfer ring to a serving platter, and spoon icing over top and sides. Decorate immediately with candied cherries and pecan halves, if desired. Yield: 1 coffee cake.

Sister's Secret

If a powdered sugar glaze seems too thick, add more liquid. If it seems too thin, stir in extra powdered sugar.

YULE STOLLEN

Stollen is a traditional German bread said to represent the baby Jesus wrapped in swaddling clothes.

If the top of this bread begins to get too brown before the bread is done, cover loosely with aluminum foil, and continue baking as directed.

1	cup milk
1	cup butter
2	packages active dry yeast
1	cup warm water (105° to 115°)
5½	cups all-purpose flour, divided
1	cup sugar
2	teaspoons salt
2	large eggs
1	cup golden raisins
1	cup blanched slivered almonds
½	cup chopped dried pineapple
½	cup chopped dried apricots
½	cup butter, melted and divided
1	cup powdered sugar, sifted
1	tablespoon milk
½	teaspoon almond extract
	Red and green candied cherries (optional)

Combine 1 cup milk and 1 cup butter in a medium saucepan; heat until butter melts, stirring occasionally. Cool milk mixture to 105° to 115°.

Combine yeast and warm water in a 2-cup liquid measuring cup; let stand 5 minutes. Combine milk mixture and yeast mixture.

Combine 2 cups flour, 1 cup sugar, and salt in a large mixing bowl. Gradually add yeast mixture, beating at low speed of an electric mixer until blended. Add eggs, one at a time, beating at medium speed just until blended after each addition. Beat 3 additional minutes at medium speed. Stir in raisins and next 3 ingredients. Add remaining 3½ cups flour, stirring until dough pulls away from sides of bowl. Cover bowl tightly with plastic wrap, and chill dough at least 4 hours and up to 8 hours.

Turn dough out onto a lightly floured surface. Divide dough in half. For each stollen, pat half of dough into a 12- x 8-inch oval; brush with 2 tablespoons melted butter. Fold one long side of dough over to within 1 inch of the opposite edge; press seam to seal. Brush each stollen with 2 tablespoons melted butter; place each on a large greased baking sheet. Cover loosely, and let rise in a warm place (85°), free from drafts, 1½ hours or until doubled in bulk.

Preheat oven to 350°. Bake for 30 to 40 minutes or until loaves are golden and sound hollow when tapped. Remove from baking sheets, and let cool on wire racks.

Combine powdered sugar, 1 tablespoon milk, and almond extract, stirring until smooth; spoon icing over stollen. (Icing should cover most of tops of stollen.) Decorate immediately with candied cherries, if desired. Yield: 2 loaves.

PIKE COUNTY PECAN LOAVES

My sister bakes these loaves to give as holiday gifts. She wraps them in small plastic bags and ties them with velvet bows.

For variety, replace the pecan mixture with a mixture of chopped macadamia nuts, chopped dried apricots, and flaked coconut.

1	cup milk
¾	cup butter
½	cup sugar
2	packages active dry yeast
½	cup warm water (105° to 115°)
6½	cups all-purpose flour, divided
2	teaspoons salt
4	large eggs
2	teaspoons grated lemon rind
1½	cups chopped pecans, divided
1	cup sugar
1	tablespoon ground cinnamon
1	cup butter, melted and divided
1	cup powdered sugar, sifted
2	teaspoons brandy
2	teaspoons milk

Combine first 3 ingredients in a medium saucepan; heat until butter melts, stirring occasionally. Cool to 105° to 115°.

Combine yeast and warm water in a 1-cup liquid measuring cup; let stand 5 minutes. Combine milk mixture and yeast mixture.

Combine 3 cups flour and salt in a large mixing bowl. Gradually add yeast mixture, beating at low speed of an electric mixer until blended. Add eggs, one at a time, beating at medium speed just until blended after each addition. Add lemon rind; beat at high speed 2 minutes. Add remaining 3½ cups flour, stirring until dough pulls away from sides of bowl. (Dough will be soft.) Cover bowl loosely with plastic wrap, and chill dough at least 4 hours and up to 8 hours.

Combine 1 cup chopped pecans, 1 cup sugar, and cinnamon; set aside. Grease 8 (6⅛- x 3¾- x 2-inch) loafpans; set prepared pans aside.

Turn dough out onto a well-floured surface. Divide dough in half. Prepare one portion of dough at a time, keeping remaining portion of dough wrapped and chilled until ready to use.

Roll first half of dough into a 20- x 10-inch rectangle; brush with ⅓ cup melted butter. Sprinkle with half of the pecan mixture. Roll up dough jellyroll fashion, starting at the long side. Press seam to seal. Cut roll into 4 equal pieces. Press ends of each loaf together to seal in filling. Place loaves in prepared pans, seam sides down. Repeat procedure with remaining half of dough, ⅓ cup melted butter, and remaining half of pecan mixture.

Brush loaves with remaining ⅓ cup melted butter. Cover loosely, and let rise in a warm place (85°), free from drafts, 45 minutes or until doubled in bulk.

Preheat oven to 375°. Arrange pans on center rack of oven with at least 1 inch of space between pans. Bake, uncovered, for 15 minutes. Cover with aluminum foil, and bake 10 to 15 additional minutes or until loaves are lightly browned and sound hollow when tapped. Remove from pans, and let cool on wire racks.

Combine powdered sugar, brandy, and 2 teaspoons milk, stirring until smooth; drizzle mixture over loaves in a thick zig-zag pattern. Sprinkle 1 tablespoon chopped pecans in a line down the center of each loaf. Yield: 8 loaves.

CHRISTMAS DOUGHNUTS

🌿 Doughnut holes may be fried as instructed for the doughnuts. You'll get two dozen holes.

1	package active dry yeast
¼	cup warm water (105° to 115°)
3½	cups all-purpose flour
1	tablespoon baking powder
1	teaspoon salt
½	teaspoon ground cinnamon
¼	teaspoon ground nutmeg
1	cup drained maraschino cherries, chopped
1	cup whipping cream
⅓	cup sugar
1	teaspoon vanilla extract
2	large eggs
	Vegetable oil
	Sifted powdered sugar

Combine yeast and warm water in a 1-cup liquid measuring cup; let stand 5 minutes.

Combine flour and next 4 ingredients; add chopped cherries, tossing to coat. Set aside.

Combine whipping cream and next 3 ingredients in a large mixing bowl. Beat at high speed of an electric mixer until soft peaks form. Add yeast mixture, beating at low speed until blended. Add flour mixture, 1 cup at a time, beating at low speed until well blended. (Dough will be soft.)

Turn dough out onto a well-floured surface; knead lightly until dough is smooth and handles easily. Roll dough to ½-inch thickness; cut with a floured doughnut cutter.

Pour oil to depth of 2 inches into a Dutch oven; heat to 375°. Fry doughnuts, a few at a time, about 2 minutes or until golden on both sides. Drain on paper towels; let cool slightly. Dust with powdered sugar. Yield: 2 dozen.

Holiday Strudel (page 82)

HOT CROSS BUNS

The origin of Hot Cross Buns goes back to pagan times when the cross cut into the top of each bun was thought to ward off evil spirits. Today, these slightly sweet buns are traditionally served on Good Friday and are almost solely associated with the Easter holiday.

1	cup milk
½	cup shortening
1½	packages active dry yeast
¾	cup warm water (105° to 115°)
½	teaspoon sugar
7	cups all-purpose flour, divided
⅓	cup sugar
1	teaspoon salt
½	teaspoon ground cardamom
3	large eggs
1	cup golden raisins
½	cup dried apricots, coarsely chopped
½	teaspoon vanilla extract
1	cup sifted powdered sugar
1	tablespoon plus 1 teaspoon milk
¼	teaspoon almond extract
¼	teaspoon vanilla extract

The icing should be thick enough to hold its shape when piped. If the icing is too thin, add powdered sugar, a little at a time, until the icing reaches the desired consistency.

Combine 1 cup milk and shortening in a saucepan; heat until shortening melts, stirring occasionally. Cool to 105° to 115°.

Combine yeast, warm water, and ½ teaspoon sugar in a 2-cup liquid measuring cup; let stand 5 minutes. Combine milk mixture and yeast mixture.

Combine 2 cups flour, ⅓ cup sugar, salt, and cardamom in a large bowl. Add yeast mixture, stirring vigorously until

(continued on next page)

Hot Cross Buns

well blended. Add eggs, one at a time, stirring well after each addition. Stir in raisins, apricot, and ½ teaspoon vanilla. Stir in remaining 5 cups flour, 1 cup at a time, stirring vigorously until dough pulls away from sides of bowl.

Turn dough out onto a well-floured surface, and knead lightly until smooth and elastic (about 10 minutes). Place dough in a well-greased bowl, turning to coat top. Cover loosely, and let rise in a warm place (85°), free from drafts, 45 minutes or until doubled in bulk.

Turn dough out onto a lightly floured surface. Divide dough in half. Divide each half into 8 equal portions. Shape each portion of dough into a ball. Place balls on 2 large greased baking sheets, leaving 2 inches of space between balls. Cover loosely, and let rise in a warm place, free from drafts, 30 to 45 minutes or until doubled in bulk.

Preheat oven to 375°. Bake for 13 to 15 minutes or until rolls are golden. Remove rolls from baking sheets, and let cool on wire racks.

Combine powdered sugar and remaining 3 ingredients; stir vigorously until icing is slightly stiff. Spoon icing into a small zip-top plastic bag; seal bag. Snip a tiny hole in corner of bag. Pipe icing over top of each bun to form an "X". Allow icing to set before serving. Yield: 16 buns.

Sister's Secret

There's no need to sift flour for bread making. Just lightly spoon the flour into a dry-ingredient measuring cup, and level it off with the flat side of a knife.

Yeast
½ Cup Water
1 tea Salt
2 cups Flour

Use my Recipe for Loaf

)16 oz pkg of Hot Roll Mix

2 large eggs
4 TABL Butter melted
¼ cup Sugar
1 teasp Vanilla
½ cup Walnut Chopped
½ cup Golden Raisins
¼ cup Candied Fruit

Coming of the Kings Bread
Mexican in Origin, and
Commorates Epiphany Jan 6

EASTER BREAD

½	cup plus 2 tablespoons milk, divided
½	cup butter
1½	packages active dry yeast
½	cup warm water (105° to 115°)
¾	cup plus 1 teaspoon sugar, divided
4½	cups all-purpose flour, divided
1	tablespoon grated lemon rind
1½	teaspoons salt
1	teaspoon vanilla extract
¾	teaspoon almond extract, divided
3	large eggs, lightly beaten
1	cup powdered sugar, sifted
½	cup blanched slivered almonds, toasted

Combine ½ cup milk and butter in a saucepan; heat until butter melts. Cool to 105° to 115°. Combine yeast, warm water, and 1 teaspoon sugar in a 1-cup liquid measuring cup; let stand 5 minutes. Combine milk mixture and yeast mixture.

Combine remaining ¾ cup sugar, 2 cups flour, lemon rind, and salt in a large bowl. Stir in yeast mixture, vanilla, and ½ teaspoon almond extract. Add eggs; stir vigorously for 2 minutes. Add remaining 2½ cups flour; stir until dough pulls away from bowl. Place dough in a well-greased bowl, turning to grease top. Cover loosely, and let rise in a warm place (85°), free from drafts, 1½ hours or until doubled in bulk.

Punch dough down; turn out onto a floured surface. Shape into a 10-inch round; place in a greased 10-inch springform pan. Cover loosely; let rise in a warm place, free from drafts, 1 hour or until doubled in bulk.

Preheat oven to 350°. Bake for 50 minutes or until a wooden pick inserted in center comes out clean. Remove from pan, and let cool on a wire rack. Combine powdered sugar, remaining 2 tablespoons milk, and remaining ¼ teaspoon almond extract; drizzle over bread. Sprinkle with almonds. Yield: 1 loaf.

CHALLAH

This traditional Jewish bread is most commonly shaped in a braid.

🔖 Keep an eye on this bread as it bakes. If the top begins to split during baking, combine 1 lightly beaten egg yolk with ½ teaspoon water, and brush over the loaf to keep the inside of the bread from drying out.

1	package active dry yeast
1	cup warm water (105° to 115°)
3	tablespoons sugar
1	tablespoon salt
3	tablespoons vegetable oil
4	cups all-purpose flour, divided
2	large eggs, lightly beaten
2	large egg yolks, lightly beaten
1	teaspoon water

Combine yeast and warm water in a 2-cup liquid measuring cup; let stand 5 minutes.

Combine sugar, salt, and oil in a large bowl; stir in 2 tablespoons flour. Stir in yeast mixture and 2 eggs. Add remaining flour, 1 cup at a time, stirring until dough pulls away from bowl.

Turn dough out onto a well-floured surface; knead until smooth and elastic (5 to 7 minutes). Place in a well-greased bowl, turning to grease top. Cover loosely; let rise in a warm place (85°), free from drafts, 1 hour or until doubled in bulk.

Punch dough down; turn out onto a lightly floured surface. Divide dough into thirds; roll each third into a 15-inch rope. Place ropes on a large greased baking sheet, and braid, tucking ends under.

Combine egg yolks and 1 teaspoon water; brush over loaf. Cover loosely, and let rise in a warm place, free from drafts, 45 minutes or until doubled in bulk.

Preheat oven to 375°. Bake for 30 to 35 minutes or until crust is golden and loaf sounds hollow when tapped. Remove from baking sheet, and let cool on a wire rack. Yield: 1 loaf.

TEA BREADS & COFFEE CAKES

*F*riends find sharing afternoon tea a pleasant way to visit and to socialize. Included in an afternoon tea menu is, of course, tea (hot or iced), coffee, and usually an assortment of savory sandwiches, sweet tea breads, and coffee cakes.

But you can enjoy tea breads and coffee cakes any time of the day. Tea breads are wonderful sliced, buttered, and toasted for breakfast. They are just right for snacks or lunch-box treats. And, because most freeze well, you can keep tea breads on hand for quick gifts. Coffee cakes add that "little something sweet" to your breakfast, brunch, or morning coffee menu.

No matter when or how you serve tea breads and coffee cakes, you'll honor your friends and guests by serving delicate treats that recall the days when ladies wore hats and gloves and "came calling" on Saturday afternoon.

APPLESAUCE BREAD

(pictured on page 2)

¾	cup chopped pecans, divided
½	cup firmly packed brown sugar
1	teaspoon ground cinnamon, divided
2	cups all-purpose flour
1	teaspoon baking soda
½	teaspoon baking powder
½	teaspoon salt
½	teaspoon ground nutmeg
¼	teaspoon ground allspice
1	cup sugar
1½	cups applesauce
½	cup vegetable oil
3	tablespoons milk
2	large eggs

Preheat oven to 350°. Grease a 9- x 5- x 3-inch loafpan; line bottom of pan with wax paper. Set prepared pan aside.

Combine ¼ cup pecans, brown sugar, and ½ teaspoon cinnamon in a small bowl; set aside. Sift remaining ½ teaspoon cinnamon, flour, and next 5 ingredients together into a medium bowl.

Combine 1 cup sugar and remaining 4 ingredients in a large mixing bowl; beat at medium speed of an electric mixer until blended. Add flour mixture; beat 1 minute. Stir in remaining ½ cup pecans.

Pour batter into prepared pan; sprinkle with pecan mixture. Bake for 1 hour or until a wooden pick inserted in center comes out clean, shielding with aluminum foil during last 15 minutes of baking, if necessary, to prevent overbrowning. Cool in pan on a wire rack 10 minutes; turn out onto wire rack, and let cool completely. Yield: 1 loaf.

GOMMEY'S BANANA BREAD

We called my father's mother "Gommey," but her real name was Leona Henderson Wood. Gommey created many of the recipes in this book and gave us an abundance of good food, loving memories, and lasting family traditions.

2	cups all-purpose flour
1	teaspoon baking soda
1	teaspoon salt
½	cup shortening
1	cup sugar
2	large eggs
1½	cups mashed ripe banana
½	teaspoon vanilla extract
⅔	cup chopped pecans

Preheat oven to 325°. Grease and flour 2 (8½- x 4½- x 3-inch) loafpans; set aside.

Combine first 3 ingredients; set aside.

Beat shortening at medium speed of an electric mixer until creamy; gradually add sugar, beating well. Add eggs, one at a time, beating just until yellow disappears after each addition. Add banana and vanilla; beat just until blended. Gradually add flour mixture, beating just until blended after each addition. Stir in pecans.

Pour batter into prepared pans. Bake for 1 hour or until a wooden pick inserted in center comes out clean. Cool in pans on wire racks 10 minutes; turn out onto wire racks, and let cool completely. Yield: 2 loaves.

Dark, overripe bananas are the kind you want to use for this banana bread. Bright yellow bananas just don't give the bread that wonderful flavor and moist texture that overripe bananas do.

CHERRY–CHEESE BREAD

2	(3-ounce) packages cream cheese, softened
1	large egg
2	cups self-rising flour
1	teaspoon baking powder
½	teaspoon baking soda
1	cup sugar
1	large egg, lightly beaten
¾	cup apple juice
¼	cup butter, melted
1½	cups canned, drained pitted sour cherries
½	cup chopped pecans

Preheat oven to 350°. Grease and flour a 9- x 5- x 3-inch loaf-pan; line bottom of pan with wax paper. Set aside.

Beat cream cheese at medium speed of an electric mixer until creamy. Add 1 egg; beat well. Set aside.

Combine flour and next 3 ingredients in a large bowl. Combine lightly beaten egg, apple juice, and butter; add to flour mixture, stirring just until dry ingredients are moistened. Fold in cherries and pecans.

Pour half of batter into prepared pan; spread with cream cheese mixture. Top with remaining batter. Bake for 1 hour and 10 minutes or until a wooden pick inserted in center comes out clean. Cool in pan on a wire rack 10 minutes; turn out onto wire rack, and let cool completely. Yield: 1 loaf.

Sister's Secret

For neat, clean slices, use a serrated bread knife to slice cooled tea breads.

Lemon-Poppy Seed Bread

(pictured on page 111)

3	cups all-purpose flour
2	teaspoons baking powder
¼	teaspoon salt
2	tablespoons poppy seeds
2	tablespoons coarsely grated lemon rind
2	cups sugar
1	cup vegetable oil
¾	cup milk
1	teaspoon vanilla extract
½	teaspoon almond extract
3	large eggs
2	cups powdered sugar, sifted
2	teaspoons coarsely grated lemon rind
¼	cup fresh lemon juice

One medium lemon yields 2 teaspoons grated rind and 2 to 3 tablespoons juice. You'll need to purchase 4 medium lemons for this recipe. Grate the lemons first, and then juice them.

Preheat oven to 350°. Grease bottoms only of 2 (8½- x 4½- x 3-inch) loafpans. Set prepared pans aside.

Combine first 5 ingredients in a large bowl. Combine 2 cups sugar and next 5 ingredients in a mixing bowl; beat at medium speed of an electric mixer until well blended. Add liquid mixture to flour mixture, stirring just until dry ingredients are moistened.

Pour batter into prepared pans. Bake for 1 hour or until a wooden pick inserted in center comes out clean.

Combine powdered sugar, 2 teaspoons lemon rind, and lemon juice. Remove loaves from oven; drizzle immediately with lemon glaze. Cool in pans on wire racks 10 minutes; turn out onto wire racks, and let cool completely. Yield: 2 loaves.

PEACH CRUNCH TEA BREAD

This tea bread is baked in a Bundt pan instead of in a loafpan. The "crunch" is created by the baked-on streusel topping that crowns the bread.

⅓	cup sugar
⅓	cup all-purpose flour
2	tablespoons butter, softened
1	tablespoon ground cinnamon
2	cups all-purpose flour
1	teaspoon baking powder
½	teaspoon baking soda
½	teaspoon salt
1	(8-ounce) package cream cheese, softened
½	cup butter, softened
1½	cups sugar
2	large eggs
½	cup milk
1	teaspoon vanilla extract
1	cup peach preserves

Preheat oven to 350°. Grease and flour a 12-cup Bundt pan.

Combine first 4 ingredients, stirring with a fork until mixture is crumbly. Sprinkle sugar mixture evenly into bottom of prepared pan. Set aside.

Combine 2 cups flour and next 3 ingredients in a small bowl; set aside.

Beat cream cheese and ½ cup butter at medium speed of an electric mixer until creamy; gradually add 1½ cups sugar, beating well. Add eggs, one at a time, beating just until yellow disappears after each addition. Add flour mixture to cream cheese mixture alternately with milk, beginning and ending with flour mixture. Beat at low speed just until blended after each addition. Stir in vanilla.

Pour half of the batter into prepared pan. Spread peach preserves over batter, leaving a ½-inch border around side and middle of pan. (Preserves will stick to pan if spread to edges.) Pour remaining batter over preserves. Bake for 1 hour or until a wooden pick inserted in center comes out clean. Cool in pan on a wire rack 10 minutes; turn out onto wire rack, and let cool completely. Yield: one 10-inch cake.

PECAN BREAD

3	cups all-purpose flour
1	tablespoon plus 1 teaspoon baking powder
1	teaspoon salt
1	large egg
¾	cup sugar
2	tablespoons vegetable oil
1½	cups milk
1	cup chopped pecans

Grease and flour a 9- x 5- x 3-inch loafpan; set aside.

Combine first 3 ingredients in a small bowl. Set aside.

Combine egg, sugar, and oil in a large mixing bowl; beat at medium speed of an electric mixer until blended. Add flour mixture to sugar mixture alternately with milk, beginning and ending with flour mixture. Beat at low speed just until blended after each addition. Stir in pecans. Pour batter into prepared pan; allow batter to rest 20 minutes.

Preheat oven to 350°. Bake for 1 hour and 10 minutes or until a wooden pick inserted in center comes out clean. Cool in pan on a wire rack 10 minutes; turn out onto wire rack, and let cool completely. Yield: 1 loaf.

Spread softened plain or pineapple cream cheese between slices of Pecan Bread for delightful tea sandwiches. Cut the sandwiches into pretty shapes with canapé or cookie cutters.

PINEAPPLE–NUT BREAD

3	cups all-purpose flour
1	teaspoon baking soda
1	teaspoon salt
2	cups sugar
4	large eggs, lightly beaten
2½	cups well-drained crushed pineapple
1¼	cups vegetable oil
1	cup chopped macadamia nuts or chopped blanched slivered almonds

Preheat oven to 350°. Grease and flour 2 (9- x 5- x 3-inch) loafpans; set aside.

Combine first 4 ingredients in a large bowl; make a well in center of mixture. Combine eggs, pineapple, and oil; add to flour mixture, stirring just until dry ingredients are moistened. Stir in macadamia nuts.

Pour batter into prepared pans. Bake for 45 to 55 minutes or until a wooden pick inserted in center comes out clean. Cool in pans on wire racks 10 minutes; turn out onto wire racks, and let cool completely. Yield: 2 loaves.

Sister's Secret

Wrap any of these loaf breads in plastic wrap after they cool, and store them in the refrigerator until you're ready to serve them or give them as gifts.

SPICED ZUCCHINI BREAD

This recipe provides a great way to use up the abundance of zucchini growing in your garden.

3	cups all-purpose flour
2	teaspoons baking soda
1	teaspoon baking powder
1	teaspoon salt
1½	teaspoons ground cinnamon
½	teaspoon ground nutmeg
3	large eggs, lightly beaten
2	cups sugar
1	cup vegetable oil
1	teaspoon vanilla extract
2	cups finely shredded zucchini
¾	cup chopped walnuts
1	(8-ounce) can crushed pineapple, drained

To remove excess moisture and guard against a soggy bread, press the shredded zucchini between layers of paper towels.

Preheat oven to 350°. Grease and flour 2 (9- x 5- x 3-inch) loafpans; set aside.

Sift first 6 ingredients together into a large bowl. Combine eggs and next 3 ingredients in a large bowl; stir well with a wire whisk. Stir in zucchini, walnuts, and pineapple. Add zucchini mixture to flour mixture, stirring just until dry ingredients are moistened.

Pour batter into prepared pans. Bake for 1 hour or until a wooden pick inserted in center comes out clean. Cool in pans on wire racks 10 minutes; turn out onto wire racks, and let cool completely. Yield: 2 loaves.

RASPBERRY–CREAM CHEESE COFFEE CAKE

1	(8-ounce) package cream cheese, softened
½	cup sugar
1	large egg
1	cup sour cream
1	teaspoon almond extract
1	large egg, lightly beaten
2½	cups all-purpose flour
1	teaspoon baking powder
1	teaspoon baking soda
¾	cup sugar
¾	cup butter
¾	cup raspberry preserves, melted and cooled
¾	cup sliced natural almonds

Preheat oven to 350°. Grease and flour a 10-inch springform pan; set aside.

Beat cream cheese at medium speed of an electric mixer until creamy; gradually add ½ cup sugar, beating well. Add 1 egg; beat well. Set aside.

Combine sour cream, almond extract, and beaten egg; stir until well-blended. Set aside.

Combine flour and next 3 ingredients in a large bowl; cut in butter with a pastry blender until mixture resembles coarse meal. Set aside 1 cup flour mixture. Add sour cream mixture to remaining flour mixture, stirring just until dry ingredients are moistened.

Spoon batter into prepared pan, spreading evenly over bottom and 2 inches up sides of pan. Spread cream cheese mixture evenly over batter. Drizzle raspberry preserves over cream cheese mixture; sprinkle with reserved 1 cup flour mixture. Sprinkle almonds over flour mixture.

Bake for 50 minutes or until crust is golden. Cool in pan on a wire rack 10 minutes. Remove sides of pan. Cut into wedges; serve warm. Yield: one 10-inch coffee cake.

CHILTON COFFEE CAKE

Named for Chilton County, Alabama, one of the largest peach-growing areas in the country, this simple recipe showcases the county's prize product.

1	cup all-purpose flour
½	teaspoon baking powder
½	teaspoon salt
¼	cup sugar
1	teaspoon ground cinnamon
½	cup butter, softened
½	cup sugar
1	large egg
1	teaspoon vanilla extract
2	cups peeled, sliced fresh peaches

Preheat oven to 350°. Grease a 9-inch springform pan; set aside.

Combine first 3 ingredients; set aside. Combine ¼ cup sugar and cinnamon; set aside.

Beat butter at medium speed of an electric mixer until creamy; gradually add ½ cup sugar, beating well. Add egg and vanilla; beat well. Add flour mixture to butter mixture, beating at low speed just until blended.

Pour batter into prepared pan. Arrange peaches over batter; sprinkle peaches with cinnamon-sugar mixture. Bake for 30 to 35 minutes or until edges of cake are golden. Cool in pan on a wire rack 10 minutes; remove sides of pan. Serve warm. Yield: one 9-inch coffee cake.

A sprinkling of orange juice or lemon juice will keep sliced fresh peaches from turning brown. If fresh peaches aren't available, frozen sliced peaches, thawed, may be used. Press the thawed peach slices between paper towels to remove any excess moisture.

Easy Coffee Cake

½   cup chopped pecans
¼   cup sugar
1   tablespoon ground cinnamon
1   tablespoon butter, softened
2   cups all-purpose flour
1   tablespoon baking powder
½   teaspoon salt
½   cup sugar
1   teaspoon ground cinnamon
½   cup butter
1   large egg, lightly beaten
1   cup milk
1   teaspoon vanilla extract

Preheat oven to 350°. Grease and flour a 9-inch square pan; set aside.

Combine first 4 ingredients in a small bowl, stirring with a fork until crumbly. Set aside.

Combine flour and next 4 ingredients in a large bowl; cut in ½ cup butter with a pastry blender until mixture resembles coarse meal. Combine egg, milk, and vanilla; add egg mixture to flour mixture, stirring just until dry ingredients are moistened.

Pour batter into prepared pan; sprinkle evenly with pecan mixture. Bake coffee cake for 30 to 35 minutes or until a wooden pick inserted in center comes out clean. Cool in pan on a wire rack 10 minutes. Cut into squares to serve. Serve warm. Yield: one 9-inch coffee cake.

Lemon-Poppy Seed Bread (page 103)

SAVORY & SPECIALTY BREADS

*H*earty, crusty yeast breads you can really sink
your teeth into—that's what you'll find recipes
for in this chapter. From the international
favorite, Classic French Bread, to homestyle winners like
Country Bread and Sister's Special Yeast Bread, these breads
are perfect anytime you want an alternative to rolls.

At the end of the chapter, I've tucked in a couple of
recipes for specialty yeast breads that can be purchased at
the grocery store but are best when made at home. In this
category, Bagels and Breadsticks are two of my favorites.
Keep Bagels on hand for quick breakfasts and snacks, but
save Breadsticks to accompany a salad or a bowl of soup.

Front to back: *Country Bread (page 114) and Breadsticks (page 124)*

COUNTRY BREAD

(pictured on page 112)

These round, rustic loaves have a crusty exterior and a tender interior like that of French bread.

2	packages active dry yeast
1¾	cups warm water (105° to 115°), divided
1	tablespoon sugar
2	teaspoons salt
1	teaspoon lemon juice or white vinegar
3	cups bread flour, divided
2½	cups all-purpose flour
2	tablespoons cornmeal
3	tablespoons additional all-purpose flour

Combine yeast and 1 cup warm water in a small bowl; let stand 5 minutes. Stir in remaining warm water, sugar, salt, and lemon juice.

Combine yeast mixture and 2 cups bread flour in a large bowl, stirring until well blended. Add remaining bread flour and 2½ cups all-purpose flour, ½ cup at a time, stirring vigorously until dough pulls away from sides of bowl.

Turn dough out onto a well-floured surface, and knead until smooth and elastic (6 to 8 minutes). Place in a well-greased bowl, turning to grease top. Cover loosely, and let rise in a warm place (85°), free from drafts, 45 minutes or until doubled in bulk.

Lightly grease a large baking sheet; sprinkle with cornmeal, and set aside.

Punch dough down; turn out onto a lightly floured surface, and knead lightly 4 or 5 times. Divide dough in half. Shape each portion of dough into a round loaf, and rub each loaf with 1½ tablespoons additional flour. Place loaves on prepared baking sheet, allowing 4 inches of space between loaves. Cover loosely, and let rise in a warm place, free from drafts, 45 minutes or until doubled in bulk.

Preheat oven to 400°. Gently make 3 (⅛-inch-deep) horizontal cuts and 3 (⅛-inch-deep) vertical cuts in top of each loaf to resemble a tic-tac-toe pattern, using a sharp paring knife. Bake for 25 to 30 minutes or until loaves sound hollow when tapped. Transfer loaves to wire racks, and let cool completely. Yield: 2 loaves.

Sister's Secret

Don't panic if you have to leave yeast dough for a few moments. Yeast dough can rest, covered, on a work surface for up to half an hour, or it can be refrigerated for one to two hours, unless otherwise directed.

CLASSIC FRENCH BREAD

Although French bread, or pain ordinaire, is a hallmark of French cuisine, it's easy to make in your own kitchen. French bread has a hard, shiny crust and a tender, soft interior. Tear it into chunks and serve at room temperature.

🐟 French bread takes a bit more time but no more effort to prepare than many other yeast breads. Longer rising times help develop the unique, subtle flavor of the bread.

1½	packages active dry yeast
2	cups warm water (105° to 115°)
1	tablespoon sugar
3	cups bread flour, divided
2	tablespoons butter, melted
1	tablespoon salt
3	cups all-purpose flour
2	tablespoons cornmeal
1	large egg white, lightly beaten
2	tablespoons water

Combine yeast, warm water, and sugar in a small bowl; let stand 5 minutes.

Combine yeast mixture, 2 cups bread flour, butter, and salt in a large bowl, stirring vigorously until well blended. Add remaining 1 cup bread flour and all-purpose flour, 1 cup at a time, stirring vigorously until dough pulls away from sides of bowl.

Turn dough out onto a well-floured surface, and knead until smooth and elastic (about 10 minutes). Place in a well-greased bowl, turning to grease top. Cover loosely, and let rise in a warm place (85°), free from drafts, 1½ hours or until tripled in bulk.

Punch dough down. Cover dough loosely, and let rise in a warm place, free from drafts, 30 minutes or until almost doubled in bulk.

Lightly grease a large baking sheet; sprinkle with cornmeal. Set aside.

Punch dough down; turn out onto a lightly floured surface, and knead lightly 4 or 5 times. Divide dough in half. Shape each portion of dough into a long, narrow loaf, tapering each end. Place on prepared baking sheet, allowing 4 inches of space between loaves. Let rise, uncovered, in a warm place, free from drafts, 30 minutes or until doubled in bulk.

Preheat oven to 400°. Cut several diagonal slits (¼-inch deep) across tops of loaves using a sharp paring knife. Combine egg white and 2 tablespoons water; carefully brush over loaves. Place baking sheet on middle rack of oven. Fill a shallow baking pan half full of boiling water; place pan on bottom rack of oven. Bake for 35 to 45 minutes or until loaves sound hollow when tapped. Transfer loaves to wire racks, and let cool completely. Yield: 2 loaves.

Sister's Secret

Unless otherwise directed, remove baked yeast loaves from the pan or baking sheet as soon as they finish baking and place them on a wire rack to cool. This keeps the bread from becoming soggy from steam that accumulates on the bottom of the baking pan or sheet.

SISTER'S SPECIAL YEAST BREAD

Because this coarse-textured bread is so tender, it is best cut into thick slices.

1	cup milk
½	cup shortening
¼	cup sugar
1	teaspoon salt
1½	packages active dry yeast
¼	cup warm water (105° to 115°)
4	cups all-purpose flour, divided
3	large eggs, lightly beaten
1	tablespoon vegetable oil
2	tablespoons butter, melted

Heat first 4 ingredients in a saucepan until shortening melts, stirring occasionally. Cool to 105° to 115°.

Combine yeast and warm water in a 1-cup liquid measuring cup; let stand 5 minutes.

Combine milk mixture, yeast mixture, 2 cups flour, and eggs in a large bowl, stirring vigorously until mixture is blended. Add remaining 2 cups flour, stirring vigorously until dough pulls away from sides of bowl. Brush or lightly rub dough with vegetable oil. Cover loosely, and let rise in a warm place (85°), free from drafts, 1 hour or until dough is doubled in bulk.

Grease 2 (8½- x 4½- x 3-inch) loafpans; set aside.

Punch dough down. Turn dough out onto a lightly floured surface, and knead 3 minutes. Divide dough in half. Roll 1 portion of dough into a 12- x 8½-inch rectangle. Roll up dough, starting at short side, pressing firmly to eliminate air pockets; pinch ends to seal. Place dough, seam side down, in a prepared pan. Repeat procedure with remaining portion of dough.

Brush loaves with melted butter. Cover loosely, and let rise in a warm place, free from drafts, 1 hour or until dough almost reaches tops of pans.

Preheat oven to 350°. Bake for 30 to 40 minutes or until loaves sound hollow when tapped. Remove bread from pans immediately; cool on wire racks. Yield: 2 loaves.

Sister's Secret

If yeast loaves start to overbrown before they are done, shield the loaves with aluminum foil for the remainder of the baking time.

MAMA'S SOURDOUGH BREAD

Making sourdough bread takes a while due to the long rising times, but you can be doing other things while it rises. I remove the starter from the refrigerator in the morning and allow it to warm up and work all day. That evening, I make the dough and leave it to rise overnight. The next morning, I prepare the loaves, leaving them to rise during the day. Then I bake the loaves for dinner.

If you prefer a strong sourdough flavor, allow the dough to rise longer.

1½	cups warm water (105° to 115°)
1	cup Sourdough Starter (page 15)
½	cup shortening, melted
6	cups all-purpose flour
1	teaspoon salt
3	tablespoons butter, melted

Combine first 3 ingredients in a large bowl.

Combine flour and salt in a large bowl. Add 2 cups flour mixture to starter mixture, stirring until well blended. Add remaining flour mixture to starter mixture, one cup at a time, stirring vigorously until dough holds together. (Dough will be very stiff.) Place dough in a well-greased bowl, turning to grease top. Cover loosely, and let rise in a warm place (85°), free from drafts, 6 hours or until doubled in bulk.

Grease 2 (9- x 5- x 3-inch) loafpans; set aside.

Punch dough down; turn out onto a lightly floured surface, and knead until smooth and elastic (5 to 8 minutes). Divide dough in half. Roll 1 portion of dough into a 14- x 9-inch rectangle. Roll up dough, starting at short side, pressing firmly to eliminate air pockets; pinch ends to seal. Place dough, seam side down, in a prepared pan. Repeat procedure with remaining portion of dough.

Brush loaves with melted butter. Cover loosely, and let rise in a warm place, free from drafts, 6 hours or until dough rises above tops of pans.

Preheat oven to 350°. Bake loaves for 35 to 45 minutes or until golden and loaves sound hollow when tapped. Remove bread from pans immediately; cool completely on wire racks. Yield: 2 loaves.

Sister's Secrets

SOURDOUGH DO'S and DON'TS

- *Do store sourdough starter in glass or crockery containers. Metal may adversely affect sourdough flavor.*

- *Don't store sourdough starter in an airtight container. Starter is alive and growing, and it requires oxygen.*

- *Do allow sourdough starter to come to room temperature before using it.*

- *Don't rush the rising time for sourdough bread. It takes several hours for the natural fermentation of the potato water, sugar, flour, and yeast to occur.*

- *Do replenish, or feed, sourdough starter every three days. (Directions are on page 15.)*

- *Do discard starter that has changed color or has developed mold.*

BAGELS

Most folks like their bagels split, lightly toasted, and spread with plain or flavored cream cheese or butter and jam.

Kosher salt is a coarse-grained salt used by gourmet cooks who prefer its texture and flavor. If you wish, substitute kosher salt for table salt anywhere in this recipe.

1½	cups water
¼	cup butter, divided
4¾	cups all-purpose flour, divided
¼	cup sugar, divided
2	tablespoons salt, divided
2	packages active dry yeast
2	teaspoons water
1	lightly beaten egg white
	Kosher salt
	Poppy seeds

Heat 1½ cups water and 2 tablespoons butter in a saucepan until butter melts, stirring occasionally. Cool to 120° to 130°.

Combine 2 cups flour, 3 tablespoons sugar, 1 tablespoon salt, and yeast in a large mixing bowl. Gradually add water mixture to flour mixture, beating at low speed of an electric mixer until blended. Beat 3 additional minutes at medium speed. Stir in remaining flour, ½ cup at a time, until dough pulls away from sides of bowl.

Turn dough out onto a well-floured surface, and knead until smooth and elastic (about 5 minutes). Place dough in a well-greased bowl, turning to grease top. Cover loosely, and let rise in a warm place (85°), free from drafts, 1 hour or until doubled in bulk. Punch dough down; cover and let rest 15 minutes.

Punch dough down; turn out onto a lightly floured surface, and knead lightly 4 or 5 times. Divide dough into 12 equal portions. Shape each portion into a ball. Punch a hole through each ball with a floured finger; widen the holes to approximately 1 inch.

Pour water to depth of about 1½ inches into a large heavy skillet; add remaining 2 tablespoons butter, 1 tablespoon sugar, and 1 tablespoon salt. Bring to a boil; reduce heat to medium, and maintain water at a gentle boil. Drop bagels, a few at a time, into gently boiling water; simmer 3 minutes. Turn bagels, and cook 2 minutes. Turn again, and cook 1 additional minute. Remove bagels from water using a slotted spoon, and drain on paper towels.

Combine 2 teaspoons water and egg white. Place bagels on a lightly greased large baking sheet; brush with egg white mixture. Sprinkle immediately with kosher salt and poppy seeds. Bake at 350° for 20 to 25 minutes or until lightly browned. Remove bagels from baking sheets; let cool on wire racks. Yield: 1 dozen.

Sister's Secret

When a warm liquid mixture is added to a flour mixture which includes dry yeast, extra beating with the mixer helps the yeast dissolve completely.

BREADSTICKS

(pictured on page 112)

These crunchy breadsticks are great as appetizers or served hot with homemade soup. Sometimes I sprinkle additional grated Parmesan cheese over them before baking.

1	teaspoon active dry yeast
½	cup warm water (105° to 115°)
1	cup all-purpose flour
¼	cup grated Parmesan cheese
1	teaspoon Sister's Spicy Seasoning Salt (facing page)
1	teaspoon minced garlic
½	teaspoon salt
½	teaspoon sugar
1	tablespoon olive oil
	Additional Sister's Spicy Seasoning Salt

Preheat oven to 300°.

Line a large baking sheet with parchment paper or wax paper. Set aside.

Combine yeast and warm water in a 1-cup liquid measuring cup; let stand 5 minutes.

Combine flour and next 5 ingredients in a large bowl. Add yeast mixture, stirring until well blended. Turn dough out onto a well-floured surface; knead lightly 4 or 5 times.

Roll dough into a 14- x 8-inch rectangle; cut lengthwise into 8 equal strips using a sharp knife. Place strips on prepared baking sheet, and brush with olive oil. Sprinkle strips lightly with desired amount of Sister's Spicy Seasoning Salt. Bake for 45 minutes or until breadsticks are lightly browned. Remove breadsticks from baking sheets, and let cool on wire racks. Yield: 8 breadsticks.

SISTER'S SPICY SEASONING SALT

1	cup kosher salt
2	tablespoons dried parsley flakes
2½	teaspoons paprika
2	teaspoons dry mustard
1½	teaspoons garlic powder
1½	teaspoons onion powder
1½	teaspoons ground oregano
1½	teaspoons ground red pepper
½	teaspoon ground thyme

My seasoning salt recipe yields quite a lot, but it will keep indefinitely in an airtight container.

Combine all ingredients. Store in an airtight container at room temperature. Yield: 1¼ cups.

Sister's Secret

There's a good reason for always preheating the oven when baking bread. During the first 10 to 15 minutes of baking, heat causes the dough to expand quickly, form the crust, and give shape to the loaf. If the oven is not preheated, the dough may overrise before the crust is formed. This will result in a misshapen loaf.

Index

Metric Equivalents

Metric Equivalents for Different Types of Ingredients

A standard cup measure of a dry or solid ingredient will vary in weight depending on the type of ingredient. A standard cup of liquid is the same volume for any type of liquid. Use the following chart when converting standard cup measures to grams (weight) or milliliters (volume).

Standard Cup	Fine Powder (ex. flour)	Grain (ex. rice)	Granular (ex. sugar)	Liquid Solids (ex. butter)	Liquid (ex. milk)
1	140 g	150 g	190 g	200 g	240 ml
¾	105 g	113 g	143 g	150 g	180 ml
⅔	93 g	100 g	125 g	133 g	160 ml
½	70 g	75 g	95 g	100 g	120 ml
⅓	47 g	50 g	63 g	67 g	80 ml
¼	35 g	38 g	48 g	50 g	60 ml
⅛	18 g	19 g	24 g	25 g	30 ml

Useful Equivalents for Liquid Ingredients by Volume

¼ tsp					=	1 ml	
½ tsp					=	2 ml	
1 tsp					=	5 ml	
3 tsp	=	1 tbls		=	½ fl oz	=	15 ml
		2 tbls	= ⅛ cup	=	1 fl oz	=	30 ml
		4 tbls	= ¼ cup	=	2 fl oz	=	60 ml
		5⅓ tbls	= ⅓ cup	=	3 fl oz	=	80 ml
		8 tbls	= ½ cup	=	4 fl oz	=	120 ml
		10⅔ tbls	= ⅔ cup	=	5 fl oz	=	160 ml
		12 tbls	= ¾ cup	=	6 fl oz	=	180 ml
		16 tbls	= 1 cup	=	8 fl oz	=	240 ml
		1 pt	= 2 cups	=	16 fl oz	=	480 ml
		1 qt	= 4 cups	=	32 fl oz	=	960 ml
					33 fl oz	= 1000 ml	= 1 l

Useful Equivalents for Dry Ingredients by Weight

(To convert ounces to grams, multiply the number of ounces by 30.)

1 oz	=	1⁄16 lb	=	30 g
4 oz	=	¼ lb	=	120 g
8 oz	=	½ lb	=	240 g
12 oz	=	¾ lb	=	360 g
16 oz	=	1 lb	=	480 g

Useful Equivalents for Cooking/Oven Temperatures

	Fahrenheit	Celcius	Gas Mark
Freeze Water	32° F	0° C	
Room Temperature	68° F	20° C	
Boil Water	212° F	100° C	
Bake	325° F	160° C	3
	350° F	180° C	4
	375° F	190° C	5
	400° F	200° C	6
	425° F	220° C	7
	450° F	230° C	8
Broil			Grill

Useful Equivalents for Length

(To convert inches to centimeters, multiply the number of inches by 2.5.)

1 in					=	2.5 cm	
6 in	=	½ ft			=	15 cm	
12 in	=	1 ft			=	30 cm	
36 in	=	3 ft	=	1 yd	=	90 cm	
40 in					=	100 cm	= 1 m